TH

NICHE
EXPERT

THE
NICHE
EXPERT

Harness the power of the internet to attract
perfect clients, publicity and opportunities

RACHEL HENKE

bookshaker

First Published in Great Britain 2011
by www.BookShaker.com

© Copyright Rachel Henke

In memory of my wonderful father,
Percy John Doublard,
17 May 1939 – 17 December 2010,
who lived life to the full.

PRAISE

'If you are building any type of business online, defining your niche clearly to attract your desired audience is very critical to your success.

'A couple months ago I felt the need to sharpen my niche focus, in order to more effectively attract the people who are looking for what I have to offer. Needless to say, this was not as easy as I had hoped – you just can't always see yourself in the same light that others do.

'After consulting with Rachel, I was able to sharpen my focus and define "who I am" much more clearly. Rachel has a gift for looking at the big picture and helping you present yourself much more effectively. This means more business and increased income, especially in today's crowded and competitive online environment. I highly recommend Rachel to anyone seeking to reach a specific market for any type of opportunity, product, or service.'

Eldon Beard
Home Business Coach, www.EldonBeard.com

'What a fantastic book, Rachel really gets you thinking about your business model and your marketing message. It's also packed full of resources to help you plan, create and improve your marketing funnel. I found Rachel's social media strategy to be a great time saver. Highly recommended.'

Elene Marsden
ACT Consultant, www.BetterActNow.com

'This book is good stuff. I got so fired up reading it that I kept stopping to implement the exercises. As a result, I discovered new keywords for my website plus I just mind-mapped a talk I have to give soon. It's getting me vibrating on the right level and ideas for my marketing plan keep popping into my head. Awesome.'

Mark Hibbitts
Author of *Alfie Potts: the Schoolboy Entrepreneur*
www.AlfiePotts.com

'Sometimes you meet people for a reason – which was why I was lucky enough to be sitting opposite Rachel Henke at a networking meeting and I randomly asked her about blogging. Her reply, and subsequently reading her book, The Niche Expert, has inspired me to pursue a dream – to write a food book – that I thought had long since died. The Niche Expert shows you that running your own online business is perfectly possible. Rachel gives you all the tools, the tips and all the technical know how that you need – and the joy is that her book is written in a simple, straightforward way and unlike so many business books is really easy to understand. Following her advice has empowered me in so many ways and although there's still a long way to go, I know I'm going to see this one through to the end.'

Anne Gould

'I loved this book, particularly the chapter on how to "Unleash Your Inner Expert". As an advocate of social media I'm always looking for creative ways to attract the right followers and gain new readers. Rachel shows you exactly how to create compelling copy that works online. Great job.'

Chrissie Lightfoot
CEO EntrepreneurLawyer Limited
Author of *The Naked Lawyer: RIP to XXX-How to Market,*
***Brand and Sell YOU* www.entrepreneurlawyer.co.uk**

'If you're building a business online, this book is a 'must have' for your book shelf. Rachel shows you how to think about your business model and marketing plan in simple easy-to-follow steps. It's jam packed with ideas to help get you to achieve your goals so much faster. I highly recommend it.'

Stephanie Hale
MD of The Millionaire Bootcamp for Women,
www.womenmillionairesbootcamp.com

ACKNOWLEDGEMENTS

I'VE BEEN BLESSED WITH MANY wonderful mentors who have helped and encouraged me along the way, as I gained the skills and confidence to create *The Niche Expert* book and coaching programmes.

I'd like to bring your attention to the following mentors and authors who have inspired me greatly and provide the roadmap for entrepreneurs to pursue their boldest dreams: Jim Rohn, Ali Brown, Randy Gage, Marlon Sanders, Mike Klingler, Joe Vitale, Seth Godin and Tim Ferriss.

I would also like to give special thanks to my mentor and dear friend, Russell Cooper, who generously shares his expert knowledge with me on so many subjects.

I'm grateful to my good friend and 'super-geek', web expert, Tony Jennings, who has helped me over many technical bumps and hurdles since my newbie days.

Thanks to Joe and Lucy at Bookshaker for doing such a wonderful job of supporting me and helping me realise my big dream of becoming a published author.

Finally, I want to thank my loving family: my beautiful daughters, Amy and Ella, for inspiring me to be the best role model for them that I can be. And my amazing husband, Sam, for his quiet strength and patient support as I follow the road less travelled.

FOREWORD

MOST ARE STILL UNAWARE of the enormous opportunity available to them using the Internet.

Some see the potential, but don't have a clue yet what they could offer, asking, "What value do I have to contribute to create an online business of my own?" Others who may be professionals offline have a general idea what they can offer but are asking, "How can I take what I do now offline into the online space? Where do I even begin?" These questions are all answered brilliantly in *The Niche Expert*. It not only helps you discover and develop the value you can offer, but goes further by helping you find the exact audience who will love to buy precisely what you love to give.

The Niche Expert is the most encapsulated and easy-to-follow "how to" book on starting an online business I've read. Welcome to the new economy!

Mike Klingler
Internet Business Educator and
Founder of Coaching Cognition
www.MikeKlingler.com

CONTENTS

Praise

Acknowledgements

Foreword

Contents

Introduction   1

   Who Should Read This Book   3

   How To Use This Book   3

One: Develop the Mindset for Success   5

   Create Your Marketing Schedule   13

   How To Map Out Your 'Internet Empire'   14

   Action Points   19

Two: The Power of Niche   21

   Keyword and Market Research   24

   Creating Your Ideal Client Profile   30

   Action Points   36

Three: Create Your Magnetic Expert Profile   37

   Your Magnetic 'Expert' Profile   37

   Crafting A Perfect Unique Sales Proposition   42

   Social Media for Instant Market Research   47

Action Points   49

Four: The New Rules and New Tools   51

   Your Free 'Giveaway'   53
   Tools for Setting Up Your Marketing Funnel 55
   Social Networking Sites   59
   Optimising Your Social Profiles   64
   Action Points   71

Five: Unleash your Inner Expert!   73

   Getting The Word Out on Social Networks 74
   The Art of Tweeting   75
   Establishing Your Expertise   77
   Social Media Sins   82
   Golden Rules   84
   Action Points   84

Six: Become an Authority in Your Niche   85

   Developing Your Marketing Funnel   86
   Creating Blog Content   96
   Article and Blog Writing Formula   97
   SEO or Search Engine Optimisation   97
   Turn Your Article Into Multiple Pieces of Content 99
   Connecting It All Up   102
   Action Points   107

Seven: Attract Hot Prospects Into Your Database   109

    Your Marketing Gameplan   113

    More Ways To Build Your Expert Status   119

    Action Points   132

Eight: Convert Prospects into Clients   133

    Plan Your Conversion Process   134

    The Consultative Approach   137

    Building Credibility Trust   139

    Action Points   142

Nine: Systemise Your Marketing   143

    Action Points   148

Resources and Links

Rachel Henke

INTRODUCTION

WELCOME AND CONGRATULATIONS ON YOUR smart decision to invest in the best investment you could make. Investing in you is your best investment.

The Niche Expert is written especially for entrepreneurs, coaches, consultants, authors and other solo-preneurs, who recognise the urgent need to stand out from the internet crowd to avoid being trampled under the 'cyber' foot.

The easy-to-follow chapters provide a detailed blueprint so you can quickly position yourself as an expert in your niche. In this book I share with you the exact blueprint my clients follow in my Niche Expert coaching system.

Working from any location you'll soon harness the power of the internet to get your message out to thousands of people; discover the new rules and uncover the new tools that savvy small business owners are using today; and embrace up-to-date marketing strategies to attract your ideal clients, opportunities and publicity.

A fresh approach is critical for success in our changing economy. Small business owners miss out too easily on the opportunities that are perfect for them because they have not clearly defined their niche.

I became an expert in generating prospects for my business after I invested in every course I found from the specialists in online marketing. As a result my business went global, fast. I received calls and emails from people all over the world whom I'd never met before, seeking my advice.

This book was born out of the shocking experience of realising I no longer wished to be in that specialist niche. What a wake-up call that was. After a few days of pacing around my house I finally stood in front of the drawing board ready to recreate my internet presence.

The courses I took and the coaching I received helped me to pinpoint my passion and properly utilise my skills and expertise. You will be spared going through as many hours of study and search as I did, only to find that your niche isn't the perfect match for you after all.

In this book I'll show you exactly how to set up your marketing funnel correctly, first time. I've avoided technical and marketing jargon but where I think you'll benefit from being familiar with certain key terms I've introduced them with an explanation.

Who Should Read This Book

There are three types of people who will benefit from reading this book:

- Firstly, those who need an online presence now. They need a straight talking, step-by-step guide to building their business online and will also benefit from seeing the big picture upfront.

- Secondly, those who are familiar with some of the new rules and new tools in this book. They are already implementing some of them, but feel overwhelmed and can see that they need a fool-proof marketing system in place to achieve their desired results.

- And finally, those who have already mastered the marketing but now want a more thorough approach to automate their systems and desire their operation to run on auto-pilot to produce even higher returns.

How To Use This Book

This is an action book consisting of nine chapters with action points at the end of each. You can read through the book and then go back to implement the exercises in each one; alternatively you may prefer to implement them as you go. It depends on your individual learning style.

Poor results and frustration come from not acting on what you already know.

'To know and not to do is not to know'
Wang Yangming, Chinese philosopher

The style of marketing I cover in this book is known by the term 'Attraction Marketing' and offers proven concepts designed to attract your ideal clients, customers and opportunities. It's always better to attract than to chase.

The Niche Expert's uniqueness is in how quickly you'll combine these dynamic concepts with the new rules and new tools. You'll effectively package your expertise and be perceived as the 'go to' expert in your niche.

It's a pleasure to share my knowledge with you and I wish you abundant success and joy with your niche business.

Yours in success!
Rachel Henke
***The Niche Expert* Coach**

www.rachelhenke.com
www.facebook.com/rachelhenkefan
www.twitter.com/rachelhenke

ONE

DEVELOP THE
MINDSET FOR SUCCESS

LOOKING BACK AT HOW I first got started with my own business it's difficult for me to recall exactly what I was thinking, but I do remember my stomach churning with nervous excitement.

I had no idea what I was getting into the day I launched my first big business programme, but I did know that it *felt* right, even if I was a little fearful.

It was a huge investment for me at the time. We'd just moved to the UK to start afresh and had very few resources. Neither my husband nor I had a job. We were renting a house and didn't even have much furniture yet. I bought a second-hand bike to ride round the village until we could get a car.

I didn't have much business experience either. I'd dabbled in a few part-time opportunities and even qualified as a beautician in my quest to work from home on my own terms, but it never grew to more than a part-time hobby income.

If you yearn for more freedom and know deep inside that there has to be a better way, this book contains the perfect message for you.

When we moved it was a natural break from the corporate world for me because I had realised it was now or never. It's too easy to get a mediocre job, or at least it used to be, and just settle for that steady pay cheque.

I knew I wanted more than that; much more.

Now I wake up in the morning and my day is my own so when my kids need me, I'm available. I could never stand asking other people for permission to do anything, but asking my boss for time off was the worst.

When I made the switch from employee to entrepreneur, I did have a head start because I felt so strongly about not giving up my freedom by going back to a job.

I see many new entrepreneurs and business owners slip back and settle into doing the work that they were not born to do. They settle for less than they know they deserve. It can be very tempting when you have a family and financial commitments; easy to get stuck in a rut.

The question to ask yourself is, 'If I don't do it now, then when?'

When will you go for your dreams? If you're kidding yourself that you'll do it next year then stop it. This is the year to make it happen. Don't delay any longer – you can start part-time.

Whether you're already established in your field or a complete beginner, you're in the right place to position yourself as the 'go to' expert in your niche by harnessing the power of the internet.

Begin implementing the action points in this book and each one will build on the previous, creating the solid foundation you need for a successful internet business. You can go at your own speed and how fast you go will depend on your experience.

Getting it done at your own pace is more important than how long it takes because this foundation will create the platform for everything you do in your business from now on, if you do it right.

That said, it's definitely not about perfection and avoiding mistakes. Mistakes are part of learning and growing so just jump right in and get started. I've made tons of mistakes along the way and I'm sure without those multiple mistakes I wouldn't have acquired the expertise that I now have.

So what is your business model? If you're not clear or 100% happy with what you're doing, now is the time to evaluate.

Discovering your purpose and passion doesn't have to be an elusive dream that you'll follow when you're 60. The internet has opened up huge opportunity for all of us to turn our passions into profits, so be serious with this.

Don't let the 'dream-stealers' stop you either. It may be people who are close to you and genuinely love you who are trying to hold you back. That is because they are fearful of change and want you to play it safe. That way they feel they don't have to worry about you.

I suspect the reason so many people, women in particular, are now dependent on anti-depressants is because they have suppressed their passion and purpose. If they had clarity I think it's doubtful they'd be depressed.

So what it comes down to is looking closely at your skills and talents. Yes – you have those too. Sometimes you need to dig deep, but there they are, waiting to be discovered.

Then you need to decide how you can bring them to the world by defining your value. Let's say your passion is to write: your next step is to decide which type of writing will fulfil you. This is where you begin to practice the style of writing you want to master, if you haven't already.

Skill and talent alone are not enough. I can sit here all day and think about how I love to write inspiring articles and how wonderful it would be to write this book, but if I don't turn on my laptop and sit down to do it, nothing is going to happen.

Yes indeed, it's the same for all of us. You're not alone. We all need to practice and you need to pinpoint your passion and purpose so that you can begin to practice right away.

That now leads us into the final step, which is mastery. Mastery is where it all comes together for you because you have practised your chosen craft for 10,000 hours.

Don't let this frighten you. You can make money and achieve success long before you've done 10,000 hours, but 10,000 hours is where you are headed if you want to play really big.

Malcolm Gladwell in his book, *Outliers*, explains how it takes 10,000 hours of practice to become a world class expert in anything.

If you're not happy and fulfilled most of the time then the chances are that you are probably not aligned with your purpose.

Don't let it stop you from moving ahead. As you're reading this book you already have enough ideas to move forward. Make sure to go through the whole book and you'll find that your intuition starts to speak back to you. You'll get those Aha! moments by immersing yourself in this process.

I've been looking for my purpose for years and it's actually been under my nose the whole time but I wasn't quite ready to step into it. I couldn't define it. With two young children I couldn't see exactly how I could do it. It might be the same for you so be patient with yourself, but step out with faith in the right direction.

Don't use not yet knowing your purpose as an excuse not to take action. It will fall into place for you as you take the first steps.

It is critical for your success mindset that you become very clear and committed to what you're doing. Throughout the chapters in this book I'm going to explain to you exactly what to do to create your online expert presence using the powerful new tools of the internet.

The chapters and action points in *The Niche Expert* can be applied to any product or service-based business, but are especially relevant for the business model where you create your own entrepreneurial success blueprint.

You can use the strategies in this book to get the word out about your business, gain clients, attract publicity for your services and products, and to build relationships with influential people in your field.

Social Media is here to stay, so the quicker you learn to use it effectively the greater chance you have of becoming an expert in your niche.

The majority of business owners are doing it all wrong online, so buckle up and I'll show you how to position yourself so that the right people are drawn magnetically towards what you have to offer, just by being yourself.

What a relief!

So many people get started in their own home-based or small business but don't take enough action to get the results they desire, so they quit. It's heartbreaking and I don't want to see that happen to you.

Whether you're building a more traditional type of business and coming online to attract more clients, or you're taking advantage of social media and the internet to create a 'virtual' business, either way you must know from the outset that a successful and profitable business takes time to build.

When you take action on all the points in this book, you will experience amazing results and be well on your way to being perceived as an expert. It is essential that you begin with the right mindset and understand that to create a successful business it takes consistency and long term vision. (I'm repeating this message because it is so important that you get it.)

Just because social media and internet applications are free or low cost, please don't underestimate their power. On the other hand, don't be deluded or confused by 'get rich quick' gurus, and think that you can send a few tweets and become a millionaire. It sounds crazy but how many people give up too soon because they thought it would be easier and quicker to make a lot of money online?

If you've been out in the trenches for a while and you're coming online to get more eyeballs on your services or products then you'll know that already.

For you, my message is one of encouragement to embrace the new rules of doing business. It can be tough for professionals who've been business owners for many years suddenly to have to learn how to use all of these new tools.

The truth is you have little choice. If you don't embrace the new rules, you'll be left behind. So many jobs are becoming obsolete to be replaced by inexpensive virtual assistants and technology.

A shining social media and internet presence is no longer an option if you're serious about success. It's an essential.

Allow yourself adequate time to read through this book and to complete the exercises otherwise you may become frustrated. It is a linear process and will take you step by step through what you need to get familiar with.

To discover how to establish yourself as an expert online, you must be clear on what you have to offer and you must have the mindset of a student who is willing to explore some new and creative ways of bringing your message to your target market.

You may be asking yourself, 'Who am I to call myself an expert?'

Well I'm going to help you with that right now.

You are most likely an expert in your field already but are undervaluing yourself.

Whatever profession you're in, I'm sure you have a vast body of knowledge and experience that millions of other people do not have.

This puts you in the category of an expert in your field. As a solo entrepreneur or freelancer, you probably already have people who see you as the 'go to' expert, and possibly refer clients to you or call you when they have a question about your services or products.

If you're new to your business, the quicker you decide what to focus on with 100% clarity, the faster you can position yourself as an expert.

There is a lot to get through but this action book is designed to make it as fascinating and fun as possible so that you can very quickly get to grips with what it is you need to do.

Create Your Marketing Schedule

It is essential for your success that you clear some regular time slots in your busy schedule to begin to focus on the marketing activities that will position you as an expert in your niche.

If you are working with clients all day, every day, I recommend you wean yourself off this punishing schedule and replace some of your hours with marketing time so you can put the systems in place which will begin to give you more time and financial freedom within the next six to twelve months.

You may need to be creative and make some short-term sacrifices in other areas to free up time, to allow you gradually to switch over to working less, and earning more with this exciting business model.

How To Map Out Your 'Internet Empire'

Here are some guidelines that will make it easier for you:

Map out the broad ideas of your internet empire with mind map software or, if you're less of a technical person, get some A3 white paper (large sheet) and with an old fashioned pen draw out the big vision of how you see your internet empire. (This is my favourite method.)

It doesn't need to be perfect and you may feel confused because you don't yet see the big picture.

That's ok. You need to just get started by putting what you do know down on paper. I tend to write some notes to remind me of what I want to research and what I may add in as the marketing funnel develops.

A marketing funnel is a combination of your website, content, system and process that generates prospects, clients, customers, buyers, media attention and/or publicity for you, depending on what business you're in and how you set it up.

I'm the most unlikely artist in the world but that doesn't stop me. I just don't care. I know that it's my ideas being implemented that bring the results, not the perfect sketch.

Draw it out roughly so you can refer back visually to this time and time again as you implement the steps.

It is easier to implement when you create your plan like this. Consider hiring a coach to support you through these early stages (well worth the outlay, if you can manage it), but if it's an expense too great you might try pairing up with someone who also wants to create or develop their internet marketing funnel. Having a 'buddy' or working partner so that you can discuss your progress and hold each other accountable to taking action is invaluable.

It really isn't as much fun doing it all alone and you can get the feedback you need by visiting each other's websites and following the process that you want your hot prospects and ideal clients to follow.

Having said that, please select your coach or buddy carefully because taking advice from unqualified people who don't have the right instincts or experience can cost you dearly.

In your plan, be as specific as you can. For instance, if you think you'd like to have a video on your landing ('capture' or 'squeeze') page – the web page where your hot prospects 'land' as a result of your marketing, then draw a box and write 'video' in it. It's a simple technique but very effective so that you can see the big picture at a glance.

There are lots of tools available to create marketing funnels and you can find the ones I recommend in Chapter Four and in the Resources at the end.

When mapping out your big vision, don't get caught up in the how. Just outline how you want it to look for now and remember you can improve upon this as your understanding deepens.

Here are some other things for you to think about when mapping out your marketing funnel:

- What look do you want it to have? Think about colours and style.

- How will it reflect your values and showcase you and your business?

- Do you want to develop it into a serious marketing funnel with a 'back end' of your own 'high ticket' products or affiliate products?

- Affiliate marketing is where you promote somebody else's products with your own unique link. When a purchase is made through that link you are rewarded with an affiliate commission. This just means you market higher priced items as your prospects travel through your funnel, which can be either your own creations or affiliate products. A combination of the two can be very lucrative and enable you to earn good commissions even before you have created your own products.

- Are you looking for a simple funnel that generates hot leads so you can call your prospects?

- Will you be providing a client service such as coaching or consulting?

- Your ideal business must match your dream lifestyle so think about how many hours you want to work, what type of work you want to specialise in and where you want to work from.

- What type of 'giveaway' or free offer will you have at your website or blog? You must offer something of value if you want your visitors to exchange their contact details with you. It could be something as simple as a checklist or list of tips. As long as it provides value for your target market and is associated with the service or products you offer, it is good enough to get started with.

- How will you communicate with your database of subscribers (video, audio and/or written)?

- How will you follow up with your prospects and convert them into clients or buyers? Will you be contacting them by email, phone or both?

- Will you set up your marketing funnel so that your ideal clients and business partners call you?

- Will you direct your new prospects to a low cost product such as an e-book so they can sample your work?

These are just some of the questions to ask yourself when you map out your marketing funnel.

One of Steven Covey's habits of highly effective people is to 'Begin with the end in mind'. This is critical for your success when creating your marketing funnel. It doesn't mean you have to know it all or even know how to do any of it when you start. It does mean that you must know what you want as the end result.

> *What action do you want your visitors and leads to take and what is the final result for them and for you?*

Then you work back from there until you have your simple marketing funnel in place.

You can then develop it out as much as you want when you see what's working for you, and get familiar with the tools and the process.

If this all seems like a lot to take in, just take it step by step and remember you can always outsource some of the copywriting and technical work, if you have the cash to invest, once you are clear on what you are aiming for.

Working with a coach or mentor who has done what you want to do is invaluable at this stage because they can help you to achieve clarity on your goals so that you can create the marketing funnel that will suit your business and your vision for your internet empire.

Action Points

1. Create your marketing schedule and allocate regular chunks of time for your marketing activities. Where possible allocate the same time each day or week so it quickly becomes a habit. Transfer your scheduled marketing sessions to a wall planner, online calendar and/or diary so you are accountable and committed to take action on your plan.

2. Map out your 'marketing funnel' and Internet Empire using the strategies covered. Allow yourself to dream big and get excited about the possibilities. You have a blank canvas to create the business and lifestyle of your dreams.

3. Consider working with a coach and/or pairing up with a 'buddy' or working partner to hold you accountable.

So, are you ready to get started? In the next chapter you'll discover the niche in which you'll position yourself as the 'go-to' expert.

TWO

THE POWER OF NICHE

IF YOU'RE ALREADY 100% CLEAR on your purpose in life then I congratulate you. You are one of the very few. The majority of people go through life not even wondering about what their purpose in this world might be.

I was chatting with my husband the other day about his life purpose and we were coming up with some new business ideas for him. He mentioned his interest in design and I remembered how he'd loved art and design when we first met over 20 years ago.

Rather than following his passion with design he went into the family retail business and then pursued a career in IT. This is what happens to most of us; I wanted to be a writer but went into banking.

We were taught to do the sensible and practical thing. I don't even remember anyone asking me what I would love to do, or what I thought I could excel in. Do you? Teachers and parents tend to ask questions about what they think you can do now. This can be a very limiting way to launch your career.

The chances are you went with whatever subject you were good at in school and somehow cobbled together a career option that made sense. It's ok, but not very inspiring is it?

I had my 40th birthday not long ago and things have really changed for me since then. People say it's not a big deal, but you know I think it really is.

It's not so much the exact age – there could be a turning point for you at 25, 30, 35 or 55... whatever, but it's the realisation that you're getting older, and that if you don't follow your dreams now, then when will you?

I've been writing a lot more since my 40th and am trusting myself with the gift of time to pursue the projects that I'm really passionate about. Showing people like you how to claim their freedom by becoming an expert in their niche is one of them, so I'm in exactly the right place now.

What place is right for you? Are you in a business that is aligned with your passion and makes your heart sing, or are you just plugging away and doing the 'sensible' thing?

If you're not clear on this it's time for you to do some soul searching. Let's say that you know your purpose is to coach women through their relationship issues; if that's truly what brings you joy then you've defined your true value.

In what capacity can you deliver your value the most effectively? Here are some different formats for you to choose from:

- One-on-one coaching in person
- One-on-one coaching by phone or Skype
- Group coaching
- Local or national workshops
- Seminars
- Video course
- Tele-seminars or webinars (phone or web-based seminars)
- Membership site – online course
- Audio, CDs, e-books
- Published books
- Printed home study courses

Which format(s) appeal to you the most? Which are you best at? Starting with the ones that you have experienced and can relate to is a good way to go. That way, you'll be enjoying your business from the kick off and combining your passion and purpose with your value.

I've listed them in the order of escalation and many people start with 'one-on-one' by phone in our coaching example, in order to gain the practice and experience of working with clients.

As your experience and confidence grows you may want to progress to tele-seminars, (mini seminars delivered by phone) workshops and/or local or national seminars. If you really want to scale it up and create true passive income you can start to package your knowledge and expertise into information products such as audios, books or digital products that can sell while you sleep.

This is by no means a strict rule of which order to do it in. Follow your gut instinct about what is the best way for you to start; this is a point at which you might consider hiring a mentor or coach to work with. Remind yourself that you are worth investing in and by becoming more successful you will be able to have a greater impact on those around you.

In defining your value and deciding which types of services you will offer you need to combine your purpose with what people will pay for. There has to be a market for it or you will be wasting your time.

It can be tiresome and not very 'sexy' to do the market research and you may be tempted to skip it. I urge you not to. A profitable business comes from an idea that matches the market demand.

By taking the time to do your research, you'll be rewarded by many 'light bulb' moments and you'll gain clarity that will empower you to take big leaps because you'll see clearly where you are going.

Keyword and Market Research

If other people are offering a related service and you can see that there are paid adverts running on Google or other search engines when you type in your search term, then it's a good indication that there is market demand. People don't pay to run adverts where there are no customers. You can see the Google Pay per Click Adverts at the top and to the right hand side of the page when you type in your keywords to search.

This is a complex topic that I could write a whole book about, but instead I'll give you a crash course on exactly what you need to do in the simplest terms possible, as it is so important that you do your research before you select your expert topic.

The success formula you need is to go after something that you are passionate about, and able to create a business around, which is a hot topic that has a hungry market to serve. This means that there are people waiting and ready to buy products and services.

If you are willing to work without making much money then of course you can just go after your passion, but I don't recommend that. Even if you're hobby focused, it is still preferable to have your hobby fund itself.

The purpose of business is to make a profit, and experts are in demand so you'll be in a position to attract high fees and be an influence for good. You can give back to your community or charities of your choice if you aren't excited by the idea of making large amounts of money.

You'll need to do some detailed market research, which will give you the foundation for your marketing platform. This will show you clearly where you are positioned in the marketplace right now, and show you the potential for where you want to go.

Brainstorm some keywords that your clients might use to find you, or that could be the ones you think people seeking solutions to their problems might type into the search engines.

Use the Google Keyword tool and type in your search terms or keywords. It's an easy tool to use and will give you a fairly accurate idea of how many people are searching both globally and locally for your term.

You'll quickly be able to rule out some search terms or keywords that are just not getting many searches or that have many searches but the competition is too fierce. You can find this information in a couple of minutes and it will save you thousands of dollars and hundreds of wasted hours.

What you are looking for is a term or keyword phrase that has plenty of searches and the competition is low to medium so you can grab your market share.

Very low competition may not be a good sign because it possibly means there are no buyers there. High competition means you may find it very difficult to appear in free listings in search engines and it will be very costly to pay for adverts.

This amazing tool shows you all of this and is simple to use and interpret. All you need is to set up a free account with Google. You will need this for other resources too as you develop your marketing game plan.

Add your possible keywords or search terms for the niches you are researching to an online notepad so you can easily refer to them on your computer desktop.

As you research your main keyword term make a note of related keywords that are 'profitable'. What I mean by this is that they have a reasonable number of global and/or local monthly searches and the competition is low to medium.

Whether you focus on global or local will depend on whether you're targeting a global and/or local niche market.

Another factor to consider is how much you'd need to pay-per-click for your advert. The keyword tool shows you an estimated price per click so you can see which keywords could fit your advertising budget if you do decide that you want to do some paid advertising.

Keep a note of other relevant and profitable keywords and sprinkle them throughout your articles, blogs and online content so that you have a list of targeted keywords to support your main search term.

Another thing to factor into your research is that the Google keyword tool is showing results from paid advertising only, so if you don't want to pay for adverts this is less helpful to you but will still be a good indication of the hot niches.

Take your keyword terms and enter them into a Google search to see what the competition is for organic (free) listings. If your keyword term is 'dog grooming', then type it in like this, "dog grooming", and you'll see the number of search results. Identifying the terms that are below 200,000 is what I recommend you aim for, but if, as with many terms, there are more than that, you'll know in advance that you'll probably need to pay to appear in those listings.

Don't be discouraged by this, the simple strategy that has worked for many is to pay for the low-medium keyword terms that are within your budget but that the competition is too fierce to rank for free.

At the same time you need to focus on getting organically listed for the less competitive but highly targeted terms, which are known as 'long tail keywords'.

This will be a determining factor in how successful you become at dominating the organic (free) listings on the search engines for your niche keyword terms.

Don't get overwhelmed by this. When we cover your social media strategy later on, you'll see how you can literally hijack traffic from sites like Facebook and Twitter to attract your ideal prospects directly to your website without paying a penny.

Amazon is a goldmine for research. You can search your keywords and find the popular books for your potential market. Many of them allow you to look at the table of contents so you can pinpoint the hot topics for your niche and see what's selling. If you have an Amazon Kindle or Kindle application on another device, you can even request a free sample with the click of a button.

Ebay is another place where buyers hang out and you can dig around and see what's for sale in your potential niche, and which keywords are being used to locate the products.

Authority blogs, articles, **groups** and **forums** in your niche can be found from doing multiple Google searches. Again, save all these links in your notepad so that you compile what is known in the marketing profession as a 'swipe file' of relevant information links which you'll be able to refer to time and again as you create your content, programmes and products.

You can see exactly where your potential clients and buyers hang out online this way too, so this market research is priceless.

There are no new truths and most of the ideas have already been used. Your job is to bring your gifts to the marketplace and to do it with authenticity and a unique twist. That is how you become the go-to expert in your niche, both online and off.

Creating Your Ideal Client Profile

If you weren't clear already, by now you will hopefully be gaining some clarity on what you intend to become an expert in. You must also develop a laser-targeted focus on who your ideal client is. This is known as your 'target market'.

Your 'what you intend to become an expert in'
+ your 'Ideal Client or target market' = your NICHE

We'll use the word 'client' but it is interchangeable with customer, business partner or whatever fits for your business model; basically whomever you want to attract to exchange money for your service or product.

If you don't know who you're looking for, the chances are you won't find them or, more accurately, your potential clients won't know where to find you.

For this reason it is essential that you clearly define what you have to offer and to whom you are offering it.

When I first got started with social media and the internet early in 2007 I didn't give it much thought. I didn't have a social media strategy or any tools at my disposal such as those I'm giving you today.

I'm sure I committed some terrible social media sins back then, but as we were all just trying to figure out this new stuff, the spotlight wasn't on us like it is now.

In my first social media 'outing' I became a paid

member of a business networking site called Ecademy.com and soon after I stumbled across LinkedIn.com. I experienced great results and was able to enroll many new members into my business programme.

I did this purely by reaching out and making friends, building relationships and contributing to group discussions on the forums. It wasn't long before I was hooked.

My life has never been the same since, and that's why my business plan and my social network looks like the world. It isn't local or even national. It is global, thanks to the power of social media marketing.

At that time I spent much too much time manually social networking which is why I've developed my social media strategy which enables me, and you, to be 'everywhere' online without physically being there all the time.

This enables you to have your social media marketing campaign running on auto-pilot in less than 30 minutes per day. Sound good? We'll talk more about this in later chapters.

In order to accomplish this you must know your ideal client inside out. It should be that if someone wakes you in the middle of the night and shines a flashlight in your eyes and asks 'who is your ideal client?' you can answer without any hesitation.

Let's say, for example, that you are a consultant and you want to get more clients using social media. You must ask yourself the following very important questions:

Who Is My Ideal Client?

Create a 'client profile' by looking at the commonalities of the clients you already have. By doing this you should quite easily be able to come up with a clear picture of the type of person you want to consistently attract.

If you are just starting out you'll need to look at some examples of people with businesses that attract you, in your niche. Study the marketing message they have and pay attention to which types of people follow them online. This has never been easier because you can access blogs and groups to read their followers' comments.

It's definitely taboo to copy their message but you can be inspired by it and develop your own message by taking into account the type of person *you* want to attract into your marketing funnel.

As I said earlier, a marketing funnel is a combination of your website, content, system and process that generates prospects, clients, customers, buyers, media attention and/or publicity for you, depending on what business you're in and how you set it up.

To gain clients you must focus 100% of your marketing efforts on the right target market so that you can fill your spots with ideal clients and not waste your time marketing to the wrong people.

Where Do My Ideal Clients Hang Out?

Working out your 'niche' can be a bit overwhelming and sometimes you will need to be patient with yourself as you figure it out.

For some it will be much clearer than others: let's say you're an author of non-fiction. It's likely that you will know your target market inside out because you'll have written your book for your ideal reader.

If you're an established consultant or coach you'll probably know exactly the type of client you love to work with by thinking about the clients you enjoy working with now. This is how your work can become such a joy, and as a recognised expert you'll be able to pick and choose who you work with and when you work.

You can quiz your favourite clients for information to help you. Take them for a coffee or ask for five minutes with them on the phone. Prepare some specific questions for them. Here are some sample questions to get you started:

- Where do you hang out with people who have similar interests to you?

- What are your favourite online websites and blogs?

- What clubs, networks and associations are you a member of?

- Which social networks or groups do you visit online?

Add this information to your market research file and be sure to visit the relevant websites to find out more because this is where your ideal clients hang out in large numbers.

You'll be able to revisit these sites and join the groups and clubs once your marketing funnel is in place, to start generating hot prospects for your services.

It's critical to take into account your specific business model at this point too because let's say you have a direct sales business and can't fulfil orders online. There is no point networking globally or generating leads from India if you only intend to service the UK. That will be a poor use of time for you.

If you have a global business or service to market then which countries do you want to focus on? You may not be able effectively to service every country because you will be spread very thin and it will be harder for you to gain a reputation as an expert.

It's a good idea to target groups of people in specific regions or countries because you can easily create products and services to suit them. This is particularly true if you want to dominate your local or national market and be recognised as an expert, although it might not be an issue if you are only working with digital products that can be downloaded anywhere.

Your business model must match your goals and expectations. If you're a massage therapist wanting to attract more clients, your clients physically need to be able to reach you, so your internet and social media strategy need to be very tight and focused on your target area.

For home-based business opportunities it can be confusing to figure out who you are trying to reach online. Take into consideration the questions above and remember that usually the easiest target market to recruit in any home-based business is people just like you.

You can talk to those people because they understand you and you can address their pain. They hear you and relate to your message and in the next chapter I'll show you exactly how to create your Magnetic Expert Profile. You'll be able to connect with your potential clients in large numbers and shine brightly as an expert in your niche.

If you are not very clear and excited about what you have to offer it is difficult to market effectively because lack of clarity creates confusion.

Action Points

1. If you're not 100% clear on your purpose, take some time to sit somewhere peaceful and just put the question out there. Ask your subconscious, the universe or whatever divine power you trust, to provide you with some direction on your life purpose. If you find this suggestion alien, talk it over with someone you trust and admire instead.

2. Go back over this chapter and create the niche profile of your dream client, customer or business partner, so that you know exactly who you are looking to connect with and where they are located. It sometimes helps to imagine one particular person and this could be an ideal client or the sort of person you would like to have as your client. This may be by city, region or even global if you are unrestricted by location.

3. Jot down possible keyword search terms you could use. Use the free Google Keyword tool to see how many people are searching and what sort of competition there is for your possible search terms. Visit the other suggested sites and compile your 'become an expert in ...' research folder. Choose the best one and you will create all your materials around that and use it as your hook or bait to attract your ideal clients or customers.

THREE

CREATE YOUR MAGNETIC EXPERT PROFILE

SO NOW YOU HAVE OUTLINED exactly who you are looking for as a client. You may have known this unconsciously or already be working with this type of person, but the advantage of getting very clear and pinning it down in your marketing game plan is huge.

Your Magnetic 'Expert' Profile

Now it's time to identify your unique magnetic 'expert' profile. Say what, Rachel? This is a term I've come up with recently because I found that my clients struggle to get the results they want when they don't understand how to express themselves online.

It's common to feel frustrated and overwhelmed and feel like you 'have nothing to say', when you're not clear on your magnetic expert profile.

Now is the time for you to dig deep and ask some questions about what aspects of yourself you want to develop and grow. Of course this must be based on the truth of who you actually are, but this is your chance to highlight your passions and strengths and move away from the things that frustrate you.

As an example I regularly 'meet' people on the social

media sites who only pop up to comment in a negative way. If there is any negative connotation in the update, they are there, twisting the knife with a big flourish. You don't see them commenting much otherwise.

What happens is that I associate that person with a negative social media profile which repels rather than attracts; many other positive people will probably feel the same.

Another example is when you see the people who only pop up to complain about lack of money. I might also see that person as negative. Everyone has to deal with financial stuff, but social media is not the place to share uninspiring 'broke' comments.

Let's say a person's business programme offers people a chance to build wealth. Do you think they will be attractive and compelling to potential partners if they talk about how they haven't been able to afford to go on holiday for five years?

Well you know the answer to that already. Being authentic with social media means being true to yourself, but it doesn't mean that you wash your dirty laundry on Facebook or Twitter.

If you're a work in progress in the prosperity department, make sure you share only your inspiring insights. You don't have to be madly successful yet. You can be a new entrepreneur and still interact effectively to bring more prospects towards you and what you offer.

Tweet something that inspires you from a book you're reading. There's a high probability that it will inspire others too.

When I talk about being broke, I don't mean just financially. You must be rich in mindset and spread your unique gifts *before* the physical and financial rewards show up. Sometimes it takes the universe a while to catch up with your vision.

If you sow increase, by which I mean add value, everywhere you go it won't be too long before you start attracting more of what you want.

So this chapter is about identifying who you are and what you want to develop into.

Here are some questions to help you to do this quickly:

- What activity do you love to do?

- What tests you the most in your work and how do you deal with that?

- What is your favourite part of your business model?

- What is your least favourite part and how do you overcome that?

- What do you love to do in your spare time?

- What would you do all day without getting paid for it?

- Where do you love to visit?

- What is your favourite hobby?

- Do you have young kids?

- Do you have teenagers?

- Are you a pet lover?

- What's your favourite movie?

- Which skills do you have?

- What talents do you have?

- Do you speak another language?

- Do you partner with a company or are you a solo-entrepreneur?

- What's your favourite genre of book?

- What have you done that is unusual and inspiring? I know you have done something. If you feel that you haven't, write down what you intend to do and then begin it.

- What do you stand for or against?

It's best to avoid politics and religion unless you are branding yourself in some way with that, but your philosophy of life can come through loud and clear online.

You can adapt as you grow, but define your starting point and be true to who you are.

The key is to be authentic and transparent.

Anyone can have a voice and gain their market share, online with social media. The old stodgy way of doing business is officially dead and your potential customers and business partners want to be able to find the information they need easily online. It is your job as a budding expert to provide it for them.

You can get started right now. Things don't have to be perfect for you to begin – all that you need to get results is a simple, one-page website that your prospects can visit to get more information and sign up for your free offer or giveaway.

Online visitors will come and check out your social media profiles so make sure they are updated and give them easy access to find out more about your services and products.

You could be the guy who tweets about books, parenting or travel. As long as that is your passion, you can provide value and find an angle to connect it up with your business. It is important that you remember not just to talk business but to be sociable on social sites because that's why people visit them in the first place.

You will find amazing prospects as long as you develop your Unique Selling Proposition so that people understand what you offer and are able to easily respond to it by requesting something relevant at your capture page. This is otherwise known as a 'squeeze' or 'landing' page and the only thing you want your visitor to do, is to leave you their contact details in exchange for whatever free offer you have for them.

If you find these unfamiliar terms confusing, associate the squeeze page with the 'squeezing' of the visitors contact details because they must enter them into the form on the page to receive their free offer.

The capture page is where you 'capture' their details and is exactly the same thing. The landing page is where they first 'land' to get introduced to your business and ideally will leave you their contact details too.

Crafting A Perfect Unique Sales Proposition

We'll talk more about setting this up in the next chapter but for now let's help you with your USP or 'Elevator Speech'.

There are many people who understand this, but a very small percentage of coaches, consultants and entrepreneurs that actually implement it by defining their Unique Selling Proposition so that they can successfully connect with their target market. It's more common for business people to be trying to serve everyone.

So being sociable and tweeting relevant information will bring people towards you, but when they arrive, what have you got to offer them?

You have just a few seconds to grab their attention when they click on your profile or website.

If your USP doesn't leap off the page at them they will be gone.

You'll be just another 'nice' social marketer, another good Facebook friend or Tweeting buddy.

As you may have already discovered, you can't run a profitable business like that. You need prospects and clients to be climbing into your marketing funnel every day. You can use both online and offline methods to steer them into your marketing funnel.

It is essential that you get your USP right so you know it in your sleep. You must be absolutely clear on what value you are leading with.

There will probably be lots of areas you could focus on, but if you try to focus on them all you will find it almost impossible to connect with your ideal clients or customers.

Overload causes confusion and your prospects will click away without leaving you their contact details. If you're out and about, this is the equivalent of what's known as the 'elevator speech', and comes from the idea that you should be able to succinctly put across your business in the time it takes to travel a couple of floors in a lift, or elevator.

If someone asks you what you do and you reel off a ton of facts and figures it won't be long before your new contact's eyes glaze over and they bid you farewell.

It needs to be short, punchy and to the point or you will lose your hottest prospects.

Here's an example of a very simple USP I helped a client develop to promote a weight loss programme.

'I help people lose weight. I lost 14kgs and 2 inches off my waist in nine weeks, using this programme.'

Do you think that would get someone's attention faster than rambling on about metabolic rate, calories and healthy eating?

That's a testimonial type USP and I can tell you that he got hundreds of clients using it. (Of course it was true, which is another reason why it worked so well.)

Here's another example:

'I show self-employed professionals how to turn their expertise into an internet-based business so that they can attract all the clients and publicity they need.'

Recognise that one? That's mine. Notice how it focuses on a few of the benefits of being an expert in your niche, using the internet, rather than the features.

Spend some time today writing down the most significant thing you help your clients, partners or customers achieve.

Here are some ideas to help you if you're stuck:

- Ask your existing clients what the biggest thing is that they got, or are getting from working with you.

- Think about what you love most about your products or service. Specialising in what you love most puts energy into your marketing that you won't have if you're just doing what you think you 'should'.

- Use social media, Facebook or Twitter, to ask your followers what they think you do. (You might get some strange answers here but you'll get some really helpful ones too.)

- Survey your existing subscribers or members and ask them what they want more of from you and why they read your newsletter or blog if you already have one.

- Test it out right away. Put yourself in situations where people will ask you what you do and just try it out. You'll soon see if you're hitting the mark because people will respond and relate to you. Your perfect clients will be keen to work with you and others will 'get it' so they can effortlessly pass you referrals.

- Tweak and repeat until you hit it right and people get it.

Remember, no 'geek-speak'. Use words that regular people understand. That way you will get referrals even if the person you are speaking to does not require your services right now.

If you're a book lover, pick books that will interest your target market. This is an easy way to start discussions with people in your target market and will also increase your expert knowledge as you read and discuss them.

If you have a travel business and love travelling, you could tweet about places you have been and places you would love to go. What places are on your dream board or 'bucket list', the list of things you want to do before you die? You could tie that in with the current deals your travel company offers.

These are some specific examples because when you have identified your targeted niche it's usually very clear what to tweet about, i.e. if you have a children's clothes website or hand-made jewellery business you'll tweet a lot about closely related subjects.

Remember never to put anything out there that you wouldn't be happy for your children, your parents, your boss or your mentor to see. That is an important rule to live by once you realise how powerful social media can be, because your friends and colleagues may be watching you quietly.

Don't get overwhelmed trying to be someone you're not and don't freak out trying to copy other people. Finding your 'inner rock star' and magnetically drawing the right people to you online comes from getting into the social media conversation every day until you feel what is right for you.

When you do it this way, you'll quickly see how your online presence reflects your core values, and people can get what you're about almost instantly. You're the 'go- to expert' for your niche but you're not salesy and in their face. Becoming good at this will make you a fortune, as long as you implement all the steps in the book so you're converting followers into clients, customers or business partners.

Social Media for Instant Market Research

How do people see you online? Can they find out about your business? Check out your online brand at 123people.com or 123people.co.uk. Does it reflect your Magnetic Expert Profile yet? If not, you have some work to do. The good news is you can easily improve it by implementing the steps laid out for you in this book. When you do a great job with this, your profitable keywords for your niche should start appearing.

Google Alerts, another free Google tool is a handy way to keep an eye on your internet presence by creating alerts for your name. You can see what others may be writing about you, and also where your own content appears on the search engines.

Here are some examples of some of the research I did on Facebook for this book and the feedback I got on my question, *'I'm doing some market research. What do you associate me with?'*

- *Proactive and consistent that I wish I was more of :)*
- *Success*
- *Determined mindset...*
- *Smiling :-)*
- *I associate a stay at home mom, who is passionate about helping others become successful.*
- *Internet business coaching*
- *You're inspiring, you've escaped the 'job' world*
- *You are a proven performer a go getter*
- *Trust*
- *Marketing and consulting*
- *Network marketing business builder.*
- *Home-biz coaching, UK goodwill ambassador*
- *e-marketing consultant for home businesses, motivator, networker*
- *You write books*
- *Great blogger*
- *Copywriting*
- *I associate you with money making online...haha*

Interesting feedback isn't it? I'm not sharing this with you to impress you but rather to show you what's possible with your branding. Never before in the history of marketing have we been able to gather such accurate and instant market research at zero cost. You can put out any questions you want to your friends or followers.

When you set up a Facebook page for your business the followers are usually much more targeted for your market than on a personal profile so that's a great place to put out your market research questions.

The answers are consistent with my brand, and demonstrate that my magnetic expert profile is performing so that people in my social network know what I offer and can refer people to me easily. Now it's your turn.

Action Points

1. Make a rough draft of your unique Magnetic 'Expert' Profile using the questions we covered and continue to brainstorm around your business model.

2. Craft your USP or Elevator Speech using the research tips and begin testing it until your ideal clients or networking partners say 'I get it'.

FOUR

THE NEW RULES
AND NEW TOOLS

IN THE INTRODUCTION I MENTIONED the new rules and tools for this changing economy. Now it's time to roll up your sleeves and get tooled up for expert success.

The first thing to do right now is to invest in your own domain name if you haven't already. This is where you plant your flag for your internet empire. Everything you do to position yourself as an expert in your niche will revolve around your main website 'portal' or 'hub' so it's important that you select a domain name that you feel happy with from the start.

This is the domain name provider I use and highly recommend: www.GoDaddy.com

Which domain name you purchase will depend on several factors:

Is your name available in .com format? If you're sure you will only be targeting one country, the UK for instance then you can buy your name with .co.uk if you prefer. There are some other domain types such as .net, .info or .co that you can consider if you can't get the name you want as a .com

If you can get the name you want as a .com and you're building a global business then I recommend you do so, because many people when keying in your web address from memory will automatically key in a .com and may find themselves directed to another website if it's not yours.

Do you have a specific business name that you prefer to build your expert status upon?

Are there specific keywords on which you want to focus and are positive you'll be creating all of your content around?

Whatever angle you choose it's important that you use a domain name that doesn't restrict you from expanding and developing your brand as you go along. That's why I prefer to use personal names – that way your website can easily grow and develop with you.

You can create individual landing or capture pages for specific products and services but you need your main domain name to launch your internet empire.

At this point don't worry about how you're going to create your whole website if you're just starting out. Just begin with your capture page. This is also known as a 'squeeze' page or 'landing' page. It's basically a simple, one-page website where you send your visitors to claim a specific free offer. Ideally, there should be nothing else they can do there; the sole purpose of the page is to guide your prospects towards your free offer where they sign up or leave.

The reason I recommend you do this is because you want to attract targeted visitors to sign up for your email list or subscribe to your database. If they don't sign up and they choose to leave, you may have just weeded out an unsuitable prospect for your marketing funnel. This is good because it saves you time and money and means that you will grow a list of highly responsive and targeted subscribers.

If you prefer a softer approach, a web designer could add a button to your capture page that says 'enter site', or 'visit blog'. This can only work if you already have a website or blog of course.

Your Free 'Giveaway'

The million-dollar success formula is that you *never* lead by asking for the sale. 99% of new visitors will just click away if you go straight for the sale. If you lead with an attractive free offer, which builds trust between you, establishing you as the expert, or solution provider, your sales conversion will be much higher.

The average conversion rate for a capture page is 20% and once you collect the visitors' email details you'll be able to market to them over and over.

Some people will sit in your list a long time before they buy anything or do business with you. If you just hit them up for a sale on the first visit you will lose out on all of these clients and future sales to them when they don't buy immediately.

If you already have a blog, or would prefer to start with a blog, you can capture visitors' details by offering your free giveaway with a sign up form at the blog, rather than on a capture page.

The right choice for you will really depend on what you want your marketing funnel to do, and to what your target market responds best.

Setting up capture pages used to be a bit of a technical and financial nightmare, but thanks to the new tools I've been using lately it has become much easier.

Now we're able to quickly turn ideas into highly converting marketing funnels without being technical whiz kids or having to outsource every little thing, which can be expensive and frustrating.

There are many tools you can use to create a capture page but there is only one I've found so far that allows you to have a professional-looking capture page up and running in one short session with no html (web coding) knowledge and without breaking the bank.

If you're starting with no website at all then you're in a fantastic position to set it all up correctly from the kick-off. The software I'm referring to provides a complete website and blogging theme (a theme is a customised template) for Wordpress.org, which is the premiere platform that every savvy marketer uses.

If you're feeling anxious about all these unfamiliar terms, take a deep breath. As an established entrepreneur going online you may have the financial resources to outsource all of this set-up to a web designer or assistant, but if you're just starting out you can do this yourself. Either way I feel it is important that you have an overview of the new tools available so that you can see the big picture.

Tools for Setting Up Your Marketing Funnel

These are the tools I use and recommend for you to set up your simple marketing funnel quickly and in the right way:

www.wordpress.org – free blogging and website platform with self-hosted software. (This means you own your blog or website.)

www.hostgator.com – low cost hosting for your website. You need somewhere to 'park' your new domain name and landing page so it shows up when someone types it into the search engines.

Optimise Press Wordpress Theme – low cost, quick and easy set-up of capture pages, sales pages, blog, complex marketing funnels and more.

I can't say enough good things about this low cost, one time investment Wordpress Theme. The short tutorials that come as part of the service are incredibly helpful and you'll be able to follow along with them step by step. Find it here www.nanacast.com/vp/97647/126367

Take a look at the capture pages on my website for examples of a free giveaway in action: www.Rachelhenke.com

You can create these type of pages in under 30 minutes using this tool with no html (technical web coding).

You can easily outsource the installation of your Wordpress software if you're a real Luddite; don't let lack of technical know-how prevent you from marketing your knowledge and becoming an expert in your niche.

These days it has never been easier to outsource or hire out technical jobs so that you can focus on your core business.

You might also consider hiring a copywriter to create your capture page, giveaway (free report or similar) and email marketing follow up messages.

Next you'll need an email marketing solution. There are many good ones but the one I find the most useful is: www.aweber.com/?367818

It offers a very reasonably priced and professional service, with advanced but easy to use features that you will be grateful for as you develop your information and product empire. Please don't attempt to get by with your regular email provider, as the minute you email more than 50 people you risk being flagged as a spammer and your emails won't be delivered.

A professional email marketing system allows you to automate your marketing messages, provides advanced tracking features, and keeps you fully compliant with the law by allowing subscribers to opt out at any time.

Once you have a big mailing list of subscribers it's a very complicated business to switch email provider so I highly recommend you set up one of the best ones from the start. Your mailing list will become one of your greatest assets so treat it with care and set it up correctly from the beginning.

If you're willing to spend some time getting familiar with the process and know what you want to achieve, there is no reason that you can't set up your simple marketing funnel very quickly with these excellent tools and services. All of these services provide instructions, tutorials and superb customer support.

You may want to pay a web expert and save your valuable time, so you can focus on developing your business and content, rather than fiddling with the technical stuff. On the other hand I have found it extremely useful to develop a basic knowledge so that you don't need to rely on a web designer for every little thing. How you approach it will really depend on your unique skill-set, your budget, how valuable your time is and how busy you are right now.

If you have the cash it may be a good idea to outsource what you can so you can be up and running, doing what you do best quickly; working on your business rather than in it.

When I found my voice online in 2007 my first blog was very plain. All I knew was that I wanted to use the internet to communicate with people about my business. The whole thing excited me so much, but I had no clue how to do it.

You're fortunate indeed to be getting started right now because the technology is much more accessible for the average person and you can have a blog set up in less than an hour.

Many people are overwhelmed by the idea of blogging and think that it must be very complicated. The reality is that once the initial installation has been done it is a very simple process to add content to your blog, so if you can create a word document or similar, you can definitely blog.

In Chapter Six I'll give you my tried and tested formula for establishing an authority blog in your niche. We will cover blogging and marketing funnel development in more non- technical detail there. In the meantime, focus on getting your capture page set up so that you can begin driving traffic or attracting prospects with your social networking.

Social Networking Sites

Decide which social media sites you will use based on your niche. My opinion is that everyone should have a presence on Facebook and Twitter for maximum visibility, but that may change as more options become available.

You can start with just those two if you are a social media virgin and haven't tweeted since the day you set up your account. Oh yes, I know you're out there.

If you're already set up on Facebook and Twitter, you can add in another one or two social media sites. Here are some suggestions for you to choose from:

LinkedIn – This has a corporate and very professional flavour to it. If, for instance, you're a coach or consultant, this will be a great place for you to be visible. You'll find lots of professionals and corporate employees here who are looking to improve their careers, many of whom have money to invest in their own personal or career development. The average LinkedIn member earns $100,000 per year so it's definitely a great place to find paying customers for your services. I predict that LinkedIn will become one of the social networking giants.

YouTube – You'll need this as a video blogging tool as you develop your internet presence, but you can also use it for networking if it appeals to you and you love the idea of the video medium for communicating with your prospects and clients.

Ecademy – This was my first networking site and I gained many valuable contacts and friends through this business network and forum. It is a great place to build relationships with solo-entrepreneurs and small business owners. There are lots of home-based coaches and consultants from the UK, Europe and the USA.

Plaxo – This isn't my favourite but it's definitely worth creating a profile and linking up your tweets so that you have a presence there with no time investment.

But how do you find the time to be active on all these sites? This is a question I hear a lot. The short answer is that I don't.

There are amazing free tools for linking up your social media profiles and it's essential that you use them so that you can be time-efficient.

Doing all this manually is exhausting and unproductive. You will need to manually message some people and comment, so you can make friends and build relationships, but you can create a powerful presence on many social media sites without being physically present very much at all.

'Tell me how, Rachel,' I hear you cry, with worn fingertips and glazed eyes from trying to keep on top of it all.

You'll be relieved to discover that it is very simple to add Twitter to most other social networking profiles so you don't need to spend much time in them and you can update the lot on auto-pilot each time you tweet. Phew, what a time saver.

Let's get started now: it's time to get yourself set up with social media tools that will have you social networking like a pro in less than 30 minutes a day. There are many Twitter applications that you can use at no cost to quickly update your tweets, interact with followers and update all of your other social networks.

You can google to see the latest ones. I use Hootsuite although that may change. Don't get hung up on which tools to use. Just get started with the best tools you can find right now. If they seem too complicated, find something with a clearer help page. I have a paid account at Hootsuite now because I use many of their professional level features, but have been using the free version until recently and it's worked just fine.

Before you can use Hootsuite or any other Twitter application such as Tweetdeck you need to set up your Twitter account at www.twitter.com

Hootsuite is a free application that will enable you to update Twitter, schedule your tweets and monitor your replies to see when anyone mentions you in their tweets. The thing that I find most useful is the feature where you can set up lists of the people you want to follow closely.

This is like having your own personal assistant who collates all the important updates from your favourite people for you. You might have a list for 'marketers', 'coaches', 'friends', 'publishers' etc. This will save you a ton of time so you can be very efficient on Twitter in just a few minutes a day.

You can upgrade for a low cost 'pro' option which offers statistics, link tracking, multiple accounts and much more.

LinkedIn and other social networking sites show you upon joining where to connect up with your Twitter account because they want you to interact on their platform using their tools.

Once you're all connected up, each time you tweet, whether from an application like Hootsuite or from your smart phone, your tweets for that Twitter account will be pinged all over your networking universe.

Ping.fm is another good service that allows you to update many social sites in one place too.

If you like the idea of creating videos (some love it whilst others cringe), set up your free You Tube account. You can do it on YouTube.com or through your Google account if you already have one. That way you access all your Google services with one easy password.

Even if it's a long way off before you think about adding in video to your marketing mix, YouTube still provides a wonderful networking opportunity and lots of amazing content for you to share with your followers so you can start subscribing and commenting on your favourite channels, or profiles, that are related to your Magnetic Expert Profile.

Adding video and/or audio to your website and capture pages can dramatically increase response, so I do recommend you sprinkle that in once all your basics are in place. Take one step at a time and don't panic.

Tubemogul.com can be used to post your videos to multiple video sharing sites with the click of a button.

Just in case you're not familiar with the term, a 'smart phone', is a phone that has applications which allow you to easily access social media and email. I use a Blackberry but any smart phone will do fine. I do really recommend this for business on the go.

You can take photos when you're out and about doing what you love and upload them to your social networks with one easy click. This is brilliant for keeping your followers engaged and for building relationships with the personal touch. As they say, a picture is worth a thousand words so it is well worth the effort and is an easy way to inject your unique personality into your marketing.

Optimising Your Social Profiles

It is critical for your success that you spend some time setting up a content-rich profile on your chosen networks *before* you begin friend requesting or adding people.

When visitors come to your profile they must be able to get a good feel for who you are so they are confident to approve your request or invite you to connect.

Use a clear, smiling photo of you, preferably a headshot. No animals or logos here. This is about *you* and this is social. It's not a corporate thing. You can add in logos in specific areas on certain social or business networks, but not on your main social profiles such as on Facebook or Twitter. Take the time to get a professional looking photo that shows you how you would want to appear to your best client. You can use the same photo across all of your profiles and this actually increases your brand recognition.

Just work on one social media site at a time and start to build up your followers and friends with friend requests. The more consistently active you are with your updates the more friends and followers will add you.

This means that your numbers can go up much

quicker than just manually adding people. You want to pull the right people towards you who are motivated to request information relevant to your niche. You will probably have several factors that link you up with different social circles. You don't want a social network filled with random strangers just to get the numbers.

Quality and niche focus beats quantity any day of the week. Just because someone has 20,000 followers on Twitter it doesn't mean that they are an expert. They could be using automated software to add people, who are probably not even reading their tweets, but are following them automatically too, so don't be fooled by that.

Focus on building an authentic network of real people, not faceless (without photo) profiles and logos. Start small and build up. At the time of writing, Facebook personal profiles have a limit of 5,000 friends, which may seem like a lot to you now but when people start adding you every day it soon fills up.

I'm now very selective about who I add, in line with the various points we cover in this book, and also because I want to leave space for 'real friends' and contacts whom I meet in my everyday life.

For that reason you may want to develop your niche Facebook page from the start, or you can begin with just your personal profile and then create your business page as you gain confidence.

It depends which kind of business you have, but for those with specialised products or books to promote, a Business Facebook page is ideal. Either way you must have a good personal profile set up to be able to network effectively on Facebook.

Twitter – moving on to Twitter, here's a quick guide to Twitter speak:

@Rachelhenke is how you would message me with whatever application you're using.

D @twittername is how you would send someone a private message. (This is only possible if the person you are messaging is already following you back.)

RT @twittername is how you 'Re-Tweet' someone's tweet. It's a real compliment when someone does that for you. Begin by re-tweeting other people's tweets that you enjoy and some of them will return the favour or comment back to thank you. It's similar to forwarding an email message, except much more powerful because the author of the tweet and your followers can see it too. This is how you start the Twitter conversation and build relationships with influential people in your niche.

This is how I registered on Robert Kiyosaki's radar. He noticed me tweeting about his book, *Conspiracy of the Rich* and his office called me to ask if I'd like him to make a personal video for my blog readers. As you can see from this example, Twitter is a powerful tool for getting influential people's attention. The other incredible thing about social media, especially Twitter and Facebook, is that you can often establish a relationship directly with the influential person whom you usually would never be able to get near.

Social media cuts out the middlemen and the gatekeepers because so often the movers and shakers reply and interact personally on these new networks. They understand it's about their personality so it can be a tricky thing to outsource and, of course, the interaction provides them with instant and accurate feedback, directly from their fans and customers.

Using Twitter is getting easier by the day because the Twitter applications tell you which buttons to press even without knowing the Twitter code, so dive right in and get started.

Don't be fearful: it is the new language and unless you want to be left behind you need to learn to use these new tools. It is simple once you decide to do it and after a few tweets you'll soon get the hang of it.

Send me a Tweet right now to @rachelhenke or post on my Facebook page: www.facebook.com/rachelhenkefan

This will introduce you to a large group of friends in my network and get the ball rolling for you. Don't be shy – just be you. It is quite good enough.

We don't need literary masterpieces, just a simple

'Hi I'm John from London and I'm reading your book'. You can ask me any questions you have there too.

The trick is to log in to your social media application once or twice a day to reply and interact, so that you build real relationships but don't waste your valuable business-building and marketing time chatting all day long.

This model I am showing you works on auto-pilot, but it comes to life when you mix it up with the personal interaction of replying and re-tweeting. By interacting with your followers you create social proof and some of their followers will follow you too. It's like a virtual introduction to a new friend.

The same goes for Facebook. If your updates are linked from an external application to Facebook, there may be some activity there even when you're not logged in. Don't overdo it and keep in mind an 80/20 ratio of social/promotional updates so you don't bore your friends with repetitive business and promotional updates.

You can choose to only link your updates to your Facebook Business Page using Hootsuite or other, if you prefer, or you might decide not to link them at all.

Set up your profiles so that they contain the link to your new capture page or blog in your bio, and ideally give them a valuable 'giveaway', in exchange for their contact details. Without this people can't join your database or review your information on auto-pilot and you may waste a lot of time on social sites without your marketing funnel in place.

You can add other leaders and influencers in your field and groups of interest, and start to add some of their followers or friends.

On Twitter, only add up to 50 people per day until you have over 500 following you. Then never add more than 10% of your following. Let's say you have 700 following you, then in line with the Twitter rules at the time of writing, you could add up to 70 that day and so on.

Adding up to 70 per day is a lot, so it's not an issue unless you're using automated software, which I don't recommend, at least not until your account is in good standing and you understand how Twitter works.

Don't use any automated friend-adder software unless you really understand what it does. It can get you in trouble and you may risk losing your account.

You can schedule some of your tweets using Hootsuite or other services so that you can automate the tweets for your free giveaway etc. This is a perfect task to pass on to a virtual assistant or team member if you have one.

Facebook change their layout and terms often, but as long as you are manually adding friends and interacting with them it should not be an issue. Again – don't add tons of people at first, build up each day.

Start slow and watch what successful people do. Keep it simple by talking and interacting with people the way you would normally. (Be your very best you at all times.)

Remember that you are leaving an internet footprint and once this stuff gets into the public domain it's there to stay, so be sensible.

Avoid posting and tweeting when you've been drinking or are angry. Lucid posts are what your followers want from you.

Always give value. This means not hurling links at everything that moves online, as some over enthusiastic marketers are prone to do.

Make friends for the sake of it, with no ulterior motive. Start to build your 'network' for life. This will be a huge asset for you in the future. Treat each person as an individual friend, not as a 'prospect'.

If you implement the steps we've covered here you'll be way ahead of most other solo-entrepreneurs online, who don't have any social media strategy or effective marketing funnel in place. As always, action is the key. Don't wait until everything is perfect – just perfect it as you go.

Technology is changing very fast so I'm giving you the big picture. Each networking site has its own rules and explains how to use it, so take some time to check that out as you join each one and set up your profiles.

Getting started does take time but once your profiles are set up and connected with your marketing funnel, they will work for you whilst you sleep – it's just like having your own cash machine.

By using these recommended tools and social media strategy, you can quickly begin to establish your powerful expert presence on the internet in less than 30 minutes per day.

Action Points

1. This whole chapter is about implementation so the exercise is to set up your tools. Start with your domain and capture page so that your marketing funnel is in place as soon as possible.

2. Create your relevant 'free giveaway': this could be a checklist, special report, audio or video series. You will need matching auto-responder messages to follow up with your hot prospects.

3. Set up or optimise your social media profiles and begin to create your social media strategy.

   To keep this as simple as possible I've designed a 'Marketing Game Plan and Social Media Toolkit' especially for you. All you need to do to access this special free bonus is to join my mailing list by following this link: www.RachelHenke.com/the-niche-expert-book-gift

THE NICHE EXPERT

FIVE

UNLEASH YOUR INNER EXPERT!

By now you're all set up with the basics. You've got your tools and have sent out some sample tweets and Facebook updates. If you haven't yet, then stop everything and send me a tweet right now @rachelhenke – there really is no time like the present to get started.

So what's next? How are you going to make yourself heard in this huge online conversation? Take a deep breath and know that you can do this if you just follow the systematic process in this book.

Look back to Chapter Three and your Magnetic Expert Profile. If you stay consistent with that, it will be easy because it's who you really are. Your followers and potential customers, or business partners, will see right through you if you're not authentic so do it right from the start.

It is essential that your first priority at all times is to build trust. You do this by:

- Always giving value. The question to ask is 'what can I say or do to give benefit to or inspire people in my network today?'

- Be relevant for your niche. If for example you're a life coach, you can build trust by tweeting relevant snippets and tips of how people can improve their life.

- Being authentic and consistent with your message so people know what to expect from you. You decide what you want them to expect from you when you create your Magnetic Expert Profile.

Getting The Word Out on Social Networks

If you're in business, one of your goals will be to make money, and with this business model you can accomplish that by doing what you love. Social media is not something to play at; avoid time wasting activities such as playing Farmville and Vampire games. If you want to do this kind of thing, make sure it's on a private profile separate from your business contacts because, believe me, it will work against your reputation and prevent you from attracting high quality clients.

I have noticed in working with my clients and business partners that a common obstacle for not being active with social media is that people often claim that they 'don't know what to say'.

It can be weird when you first start out because it is a new and unfamiliar environment, however it is very easy to get to the stage where you feel comfortable sharing tips and giving value online, as long as you do a little bit every day.

It's exactly the same as any other area of your business that you need to master. If you only follow up with potential clients or prospects once a month, then of course you are not going to be the best you can be at this.

Participating in social media every day, even for 30 minutes, will soon bring you to the point where you are making exciting friendships and potential JVs (joint ventures) with other leaders who share the same target market as you. You'll also be attracting your ideal clients to review what you have to offer.

I'm going to give you some ninja copywriting and content tips to get you networking like a rock star right away.

These things are simple but very effective and if you implement them consistently you will get great results. I guarantee it.

The Art of Tweeting

Twitter is a marketer's dream tool when used right. You don't even have to be able to write a lot. In fact you must focus on being effective in less than 140 characters. I recommend writing even shorter tweets to encourage people to 'Re-Tweet' them. They won't do that if your tweet is too long because it will go over the 140 character mark once it adds their @name and/or comment.

So short but relevant tweets are the name of the game, but they must be relevant to your niche so you attract the right people to follow you.

- Use a smart phone, if possible, to update Twitter when you're not online. (I use a Blackberry but any smart phone will do just fine)

- Use search.twitter.com to find people in your target market and key influencers in your niche. Send them a tweet and Re-Tweet their tweets so they notice you.

- Whenever something interesting, inspiring or educational for your niche happens, ask yourself how you can turn it into a tweet. If you need more space, use Facebook updates instead but get it out there into the social media conversation while you're inspired (takes 30 seconds – it's not an essay).

- Have an open mind and begin looking for opportunities that will motivate you to inspire your followers. Reading books, listening to audios, watching videos, reading e-books and reports, working with clients, talking to your business partners, networking on and offline will give you abundant content to tweet about, to name just a few sources.

Establishing Your Expertise

To be an expert in your niche you must immerse yourself and then you will never run out of relevant information to share. It's easy when you approach it like this. As you develop and discover, you in turn help your followers to do the same. We learn better by teaching so it's a real win-win.

- Pop into your Twitter application and Facebook to see who has been commenting on, or replying to your updates. I recommend doing this twice a day. More than that and you will probably be spending too much time away from your core business activities.

- Ensure your capture page link figures prominently on your profiles in your bio or information section.

- Tweet intriguing questions or tips and include a direct link to your special report, video, or latest blog post, which will either answer the question or give them more tips. It must be relevant and value based.

- Tweet about the highlights not the lowlights of your day.

It's easy to forget that if you have your Tweets linked to other social sites (I do recommend this unless you are doing hundreds of tweets per day) you may very well be generating conversations at the other sites you link to, so remember to check in with those every so often too.

This is truly wonderful and serves as a perfect example of time leverage. You're not even there, and potential clients and customers can be over on your profile reading about you and joining your mailing list or database.

This increases the synergy between you and your followers, builds the relationship of trust, and of course points them to the information to put them in the right mindset to do business with you.

You can position yourself very quickly as an expert in your niche, or if that seems too grand for you now, as an authority in your niche.

Even if you just started your business today you can already make the decision to be a serious professional, so from day one you must use social media responsibly because people will be watching you.

Social networking is an art. The great news is that you can get better at it as you practise so don't be fazed by that. As you're reading this, you're already committed to your personal development so all you need to do to be successful with social media is to take the high points of each day and turn them into several useful tweets or updates.

Don't let a day pass without doing this. Even if you don't work on a Saturday or Sunday, you can still do a couple of non work-related updates. Tweet about your gratitude for a wonderful day with your family or tweet something inspiring about what you are doing that day.

You can send out your special report link too, as many of your prospects will have more free time to download and read it at the weekend. This can be scheduled in advance to go out over the weekend or holidays.

You don't even need to go near your computer if you get connected with a smart phone.

I'm going to give you a tip right now that will save you lots of time and make it very easy to promote your business more directly.

Many people will click on your website link as long as it's displayed prominently on your profiles with a compelling tag line or call to action, but to speed things along you can also be more proactive. As soon as you start tweeting, begin to keep a 'swipe file' or notepad of your best promotional tweets.

Don't tweet business links more than a couple of times a day, but as long as you are giving out good stuff with no links most of the time, you can share your business links some of the time.

As I mentioned already I use an 80/20 formula so 80% tweeting inspirational, social or relevant tips for my target market and 20% promotional links to my business programmes or products.

Keep a copy of your favourite and most effective tweets and re-use them and improve upon them over time. You'll soon see by the results you get and you can also track the click response with Hootsuite or other Twitter tools for a more accurate test.

This works best when you're promoting an 'evergreen' programme or product, meaning that it doesn't change often and is one of your core services or products.

It's a great way for getting new people started as affiliates for your product or joint venture partners in your business. As long as you explain to them how the 80/20 rule works they'll be good to go and can personalise your tweets by adding on their own affiliate website link instead of yours.

Better yet, have them invest in their own copy of this book so they too can discover the secrets of social media networking and set up their business foundation correctly right from the start.

Social media can really work for all personality types. If you're an outgoing socialite you'll love the opportunity to interact with all your friends and colleagues with just the click of a button.

If you're a shy pussycat, social media can be a blessing for you as you can begin to broaden your network and grow your business from the comfort of your home. When you've had enough for the day, you can retire elegantly to lick your silky paws...

It's always a good idea to stretch yourself and make the effort to network offline too, but once you've tried both forms of networking you'll soon know which works best for you and which you want to invest the most time in doing.

I adore social media and it has opened up partnerships, international markets and opportunities for me that I never would have had access to if I was only doing local or national networking.

This demonstrates the power of online networking, but person to person networking basics will *never* go out of fashion so whether you are focusing on your local market or you have a 'no borders business', don't ignore offline networking because you may miss out on some excellent strategic alliances and clients.

The partnerships and relationships that develop from meeting in person are often the most valuable, so even if you love working in your pyjamas with just an internet connection, I still recommend attending suitable events even if it's just to meet possible joint venture partners.

Always go for getting exposure in 100% of your market, not just 50%, by being only present online. And remember to conduct your offline networking and social media marketing by always coming from a place of adding value.

This is the mindset you must cultivate to be successful. Otherwise you risk coming across like a cold caller trying to thrust products and services on to people who are not looking for them.

As we continue through this book you'll learn lots more strategies and tips about how to be effective online but let's start with the 10 things you must *never* do if you don't want to be a social outcast.

These social media sins are right up there with going to dinner with friends and trying to enroll your hostess into your new programme, as she dishes out the prawn cocktail.

They're as bad as 'selling' people on your products at a cocktail party, and sticking your business card in people's faces whilst they're trying to sip their margaritas.

Yes they are just that bad.

Thou Shalt Not Commit The Following Social Media Sins!

1. Post (spam) your website links on to people's social media profiles, groups or forums.

2. Add people to your social network with a message to say they must check out your amazing business (seriously – I get tons of these and they are such a turn off).

3. Add people manually to your groups without first asking their permission.

4. Randomly tag people in your Facebook posts that have nothing to do with them.

5. Whine and talk about someone else in a negative way. If you have a disagreement, take it off the public profiles immediately and settle it privately.

6. Be dull and boring.

7. Use pictures of animals or your product as your profile picture. Serious business people do not want to friend products or animals online.

8. Interact online when you are inebriated (tipsy).

9. Interact online when you are angry. Walk away.

10. Put anything out there that you wouldn't want all to see.

By being aware of these social media sins you'll be able to shine online and start reaping the rewards of social media networking.

The great news is that you can be heard and get your compelling message out there to the people you want to reach by simply being *you*. Yes, just be authentic and aligned with who you are and what you are working to accomplish.

If you combine this with good social media etiquette, which is very similar to regular good manners, you will be successful in growing a large, supportive network of friends and raving fans that will help you spread your expert message all over the internet.

Golden Rules

Always keep these social media sins in mind or you will be labeled as an amateur rather than an expert.

The only way you won't be successful is if you don't contribute consistently. But then that's the same with most things, isn't it?

It's not so much the truly talented who consistently do well, but usually the real *doers*.

Whatever your personality, as long as you are aligned with your ideal business model and you're clear on your Magnetic Expert Profile, you will thrive with social media.

You've already done all the work for your profile in Chapter Three, so now you can unleash your inner expert and begin attracting the right people into your marketing funnel, inexpensively and in large numbers.

Action Points

1. Practise tweeting and updating your social networks using the tips we covered.

2. Begin or continue adding friends and relevant connections on your social networks.

3. Craft some tweets for your main free giveaway and either schedule them or manually tweet them a couple of times a day, keeping in mind the 80/20 rule.

SIX

BECOME AN AUTHORITY IN YOUR NICHE

THIS CHAPTER IS ABOUT ATTRACTING the perfect people to you by positioning yourself online as an expert in your niche and building your brand. Read on, because this can lead to new friends, free gifts, joint venture partners, large commissions, high coaching fees, business opportunities, publishing offers, more clients, affiliates, or even a buyer for your house.

When used well, social media and the internet open up the world for you and enable you to be everywhere at once. Just a couple of years ago business owners could only dream of this kind of leverage. Now it's a reality and you can get your message out at no cost as far and as wide as suits your niche.

Once you've mastered the basics, which doesn't take long, I recommend you master Twitter and Facebook first, before adding in other sites, so that you don't fall into the overwhelm trap.

In Chapter Four we covered the basics of getting set up with your marketing tools. By now you should have implemented those steps and at least have your one-page website and basic marketing funnel in place. If you're stuck and not implementing what you have learned in the chapters, ask yourself what's holding you back.

My guess is that you're either not yet clear on the niche in which you want to become an expert, or perhaps you're overwhelmed by the thought of creating your marketing funnel.

Please don't let either of these obstacles stop you from moving forward in creating your dream business and lifestyle. Everyone needs a mentor to play a bigger game and you can't do everything all on your own.

It is essential that you have clarity on which niche you will focus on, because if you create a game plan around something you are not very passionate about, you will probably run out of steam and not be sufficiently inspired to take enough action.

Making changes and creating a new business takes courage. When you map out an exciting game plan that you believe in, you'll be so inspired that your courage will not fail you.

Developing Your Marketing Funnel

Now we're going into more detail about how to set up and develop your marketing funnel so that you stand out as a true expert in your niche, with your own powerful brand.

To get great results, you need to be in action today, not in two weeks or two months... when your marketing funnel is 'perfect'.

If you have no website, blog or capture page, then get that up and running as quickly as you humanly can, otherwise you're marketing with a leaky bucket or with no bucket.

Perfect your funnel as you go. One of my clients has a 24% conversion rate from visitor to lead sign up with just one page offering a free report and a simple form to collect her visitors' contact details.

The free application called Wordpress which I mentioned earlier has turned the online marketing world on its head. Before Wordpress it was harder to have more than a simple blog, unless we were experts in technical set up and website design or were willing to pay someone who was.

The benefits of the Wordpress.org platform are numerous and too many to mention here, but the main one is that you can now easily create and update your own website and blog so you are not dependent on any other source to maintain it. You also own your domain name and that is where the blog is parked.

Wordpress is 'open source', which means that you have an abundant supply of 'plugins' that give increased functionality and endless options for blog and website layout and features. If you're like me you may not use them to their full capabilities but you can develop your funnel as you and your business grow.

You can use a free theme if it's just a simple Wordpress blog that you want, or you can create a whole website on this platform, which I recommend for all budding experts.

There are some other types of blogging platforms which you may already have heard of or be using: WordPress.com and Blogger.com are popular examples of these. They are completely free and you can set them up in a couple of minutes which is very cool. My teenagers have blogs of this type.

The downside of these is that you don't own your blog. This means, for instance, that Google hosts Blogger so you don't get full control over what will be available on it. You can, however, purchase your own domain name and redirect it to the sub-domain provided by the platform if you wish.

This can work well if you just want to give blogging a go, so you could purchase your own domain name, such as JohnGalt.com, and quickly forward it to point at the blog so that you have an easier and more attractive blog name, rather than the longer, difficult to remember, johngalt.blogspot.com. Do you see?

This is only suitable if you don't want to create a website around your blog. Many writers use Blogger or Wordpress.com but I fear they don't understand that their site is completely out of their control and could be closed down at any time. Google and Wordpress change their terms and conditions often and there have been many cases where people have had their blogs removed when posting something that doesn't meet with the latest regulations. If you're serious about creating your own 'online real estate,' which, as you're reading this book, I think you probably are there is really only one option. This keeps things nice and simple.

For that reason anything specific to do with websites that I refer to from now on will be related to the Wordpress.org platform, but the marketing principles will be the same for any website.

At this point, if you haven't set up your basic marketing funnel pop back to Chapter Four where all the automated tools I use and recommend are listed. You can also find them at the end of the book in the Resources section.

So you have your one-page website, which may just be a capture page, set up and ready to go. You'll need it to be connected up to your email auto-responder so that when someone subscribes at your page, they receive a welcome email and a link to whatever it is you are giving them.

This is known as an ethical bribe or free giveaway. You must have something to give away that your target market wants, otherwise they won't leave their details.

If you're not much of a writer, don't worry. It could be something as simple as a one-page checklist or it could be an interview with another expert in your niche.

There are a million and one options for things you can give away so don't get overwhelmed or stuck on this. Here are some popular options:

- A special report – from five to 30 pages long
- A checklist of 'what to do to achieve...'
- An e-course or tips delivered by email
- An audio download of a recorded interview
- Access to a video course or tips
- A free e-book
- A physical CD
- A physical newsletter

You can create something yourself or pay someone else to create it for you, which is another example of outsourcing. The trick is to get something up there as quickly as possible even if it's a short report. As long as it is relevant and compelling for your target market, people will happily exchange their contact details to claim it from you.

In Wordpress there is a wonderful blogging function which is the feature I recommend you set up after your capture page. If you're already blogging with Wordpress, then just create a new page for your capture page as this is how you will start to develop your authority website around your blog.

You can have a link or button on your home or front page that allows visitors to access your blog and website even if they don't subscribe to your free offer at first look.

I favour that approach on the home page, but I wouldn't give other clicking options on dedicated capture pages as they convert best when there are no distractions. For your main website it's good to let first time visitors have a click around and see what you're all about.

Your opt-in box (sign up form) needs to be visible on all pages of your website and blog. The easiest way to do this is to create a web form in your email auto-responder service. This takes just a few seconds and then you pop the code that is generated, into a 'text widget' in Wordpress.

Widgets are wonderful and you can get the code from your favourite social media applications and put those on your blog too. For instance when you create your Facebook Business Page you'll be able to generate some code for a widget and put that on your website and blog so your readers can find you on Facebook and join your community.

For real life examples, just visit my website at: www.rachelhenke.com and also keep a note of other websites that you like the look of.

I develop my marketing funnel as new things

become available but the way it is set up is a solid formula for you to model. Please don't copy my pages – just model and adapt them for your niche, to create your own. It's essential that you be authentic and original with your style so you can stand out as an expert and not a 'copy cat' marketer.

I recommend Optimise Press as your Wordpress theme as it enables you to have as many professional looking capture and sales pages as you want on the same domain and website.

If you already have a Wordpress theme on your site and don't want to start again, you can install Optimise Press in a sub directory of your blog so that you can create pages more easily as you develop your offers and products. The tutorials in Optimise Press show you exactly how to do this and it isn't half as complicated as it sounds. Ask a web assistant or designer to install this for you if the thought of it is making your hair stand on end.

If you're starting out right now it's ideal because you or your web designer can just install it as your Wordpress theme and you'll be able to create an amazing website and blog without paying thousands for web design.

So now it's shaping up. You have your basic marketing funnel, free giveaway and blog in place.

Just in case you're dreading the idea of blogging and need some more encouragement, here are some of the key reasons why a blog is absolutely essential for you to position yourself as an expert online:

- Blogs are cool and every business should have one. Why? Blogs are easy to set up and maintain. They provide one of the easiest ways for you to brand you and your business online and to get free, qualified traffic to your websites.

- Google loves blogs and ranks them highly. Google my name and you will find my blog immediately. This builds credibility and, because of the personalised content on blogs, people seem to trust the message more, and enjoy reading more than on regular websites. Note: you must provide quality content – not bash your readers over the head with opportunities. Visitors are looking for information and solutions.

- Your blog is completely in your control. Never before have we had such an opportunity to personally brand ourselves and be in control of our own marketing message without paying hundreds and thousands of pounds or dollars for the privilege.

- You can learn to make short videos or you can paste other people's videos on to your blog posts where appropriate to your niche, which provide residual value and traffic. It is wonderful because you do the work once but will generate traffic to your blog or website over and over.

- All the content you produce can be re-formatted into a different delivery method so, for instance, you can write a 500 word article for your blog on Monday. On Tuesday you can create a short video with the same message which will appeal to more 'visual' types who are searching for video training. Then you can submit your article to a few good article directories such as ezinearticles.com, articlesbase.com or amazines.com. Do you understand the power of this? It means that you only have to think about this once and do a little planning, and then you can use the same information repeatedly.

- A blog is interactive and is an essential part of the new social media marketing tools. People no longer expect to be preached to by stiff looking television presenters with monotone voices, or taken for idiots by newspaper reporters. They want to be a part of the communication and able to have their say. They can have their voice by commenting on your blog as it's a two-way street.

- Blogging is the easiest way to add new content to your website. This means your website will be ranked higher by Google because search engines love frequently updated websites.

- When you create all of your content around a set of keywords or search terms that are specific for your niche or target market, you will automatically become an online expert in your niche.

- Once your blog is installed, it is as simple as any word processing or email application to use, so if you can email or type a Word document you can be a blogger.

These are just a few of the reasons why you will want to take advantage of blogging technology. By now you should be asking yourself, 'Why would I not have a blog?'

If you're concerned about writing content, don't be. You don't need to be Shakespeare to blog. The people you want to attract are hungry for the answers that you have. As an expert in your niche, you already have hundreds of related topics you can write about.

Creating Blog Content

Here is my content creation formula that enables me never to run out of content ideas for my blog, and has established it as a high-ranking authority blog in my niche.

Buy a notepad or use an online notepad so that you can jot down ideas as they come to you when you're busy with other things.

Don't wait for your blogging day to begin thinking about what you'll write about. Plan in advance so that you can just begin creating your post.

As you go about your daily work with clients, or doing whatever it is you do in your business, keep notes of any ideas or relevant topics that come to mind.

Keep a list of questions that you're asked in your business. You can easily turn a question into a blog post by answering it in a little bit of detail. Your readers will often have the same questions as each other so this is really powerful.

Before you begin your first blog take a few minutes to jot down all the topics or sub-niches that are relevant to your main niche. Add to this list often, so you never run out of things to blog about.

Aim to create a blog post at least once a week; two to three times a week will give better results, at least in the beginning when you're launching your blog and want it to be picked up by search engines.

If you don't have time for more than once a week

that is a great start. Fifty two posts a year will be enough for your first book about your niche. Don't underestimate the power of one blog post per week.

Article and Blog Writing Formula

Use a clock or stopwatch and give yourself just 30 minutes to write as much as you can. Just get it down in Word or another word-processing application and don't worry about it being perfect.

Choose a title such as 'Seven Ways to...', '10 Reasons to...', 'Five Top Tips for...'.

Sprinkle your top keywords or search terms that are relevant to your niche throughout the article and in the title too where possible. Don't put too many in and just do it where it naturally flows.

In the case of a real estate or property expert, they might sprinkle the term 'real estate professionals training', throughout their articles and content. If you haven't done your market research yet and pinpointed your profitable keywords using the keyword tool, now is definitely the time to go back and do that.

All your content will revolve around your niche keywords so that your target market can easily find you in searches they perform online.

SEO or Search Engine Optimisation

If you use random keywords and don't develop a strong presence for your core keywords, your ideal clients and customers won't be able to find you. This is so important and is known as SEO or Search Engine Optimisation.

You can get really good at this even if you are not at all technical, so stay with me here. As long as you identify your keywords and search terms (one main niche and several related keywords works just fine) you will always know what to write about because you'll create content around your niche and these search terms.

For a successful article or blog post jot down a note before you start, briefly outlining the introduction, body of the article and a summary. It's an easy formula and will stop you from rambling.

People don't have time to read very long articles, so short and to the point articles work best. Five hundred words is a good average because then you'll be able to use the article for article directories without adding to it.

Make your introduction compelling by asking a question, or addressing a common problem for your reader.

Then answer it in the body, using facts and examples or a personal story.

The summary wraps it all up and leads the reader into taking further action. Here you can prompt them to download your free report or audio etc.

That's all you need to do to create quality content for your blog or website.

Turn Your Article Into Multiple Pieces of Content

Write a short but original article of approximately 500 words.

Use it as your 'article of the week' in your newsletter or ezine (electronic magazine) which is just a newsletter delivered by email.

Post it on your blog and file it in a category related to the main keywords or topic.

Submit it to free article directories a few days later, so the search engines have time to index your blog first. My favourite one is ezinearticles.com, which positions you as an expert author so is a perfect match for what we want to accomplish.

Connect your blog with a Facebook application called Networked Blogs. Just search for it on Facebook and add your blog. Each time you post to your blog, Facebook will automatically create a note from your article. This will be published to your home feed on Facebook and encourage new readers to follow your blog. Sweet.

Create a short video explaining the main points of your article. Just use the introduction, body and summary for a two to three-minute video. Upload it to video hosting sites. You Tube and Viddler are the ones I use most.

Create an audio: there are various software options for this so just use a Google search to find what appeals to you. The goal is to have an MP3 recording which you can post on your website and/or send out to your email subscribers.

Offer your article to niche print and online magazines and trade publications.

As you can see, there are many options for you to repurpose the same content so you save time and automate your marketing. Choose a couple of options to get started and try new things as you go.

If you're thinking that you don't have the face, or the desire to be a YouTube 'guru', don't fret. You can blog quite happily without producing your own videos if that's not your thing. As with all of these new tools, you may find that once you master one method, the others won't seem quite so daunting.

It's all about baby steps and gaining confidence so, as I often say, you just need to get started. If you already have a blog but are not blogging because it seems too difficult to start, use my tips, and also google some other authority blogs in your industry to get more ideas.

Wherever you submit your content, remember to always include your relevant niche keywords so that you can begin to come up in search engines as an expert in your niche.

Once your website/blog ranks with a Google page rank of three or four, you are officially an authority website. Keep adding content consistently and encouraging readers to comment on your blog. This adds to your credibility and helps with your blog ranking.

When people in the media or those with connected niches are looking for other experts to quote, you show up in the search engines. You can Google search for the Google page rank bar, and install it easily so you can track your ranking as time goes on.

This is not an overnight strategy, which is why I talk so much about getting clear on your niche because if you switch around often you'll never reach authority website status.

There are quicker ways of positioning yourself as an expert, many of which we've already covered, but this is a long term strategy that will give you a real asset and will be your online 'real estate', and steady traffic generator for years to come.

As you attract more and more people from your target market towards you via your website and blog – or 'marketing hub', as it's sometimes called -- you'll attract all kinds of wonderful opportunities too.

I and others I have coached have made influential new friends all over the world, received free gifts, partnered with other experts, earned commissions on their niche products, coaching fees, copywriting projects, clients, affiliates and, best of all, wonderful feedback and thanks from readers, partners and clients.

All of these things create credibility and brand recognition.

Here are some more things for you to add into the mix as you build your marketing funnel and develop your brand.

As recommended in Chapter Two, test your USP, or Unique Sales Proposition, before you create all your marketing materials and web pages.

Once you're clear on your USP or Elevator Speech, you can go ahead and begin creating your materials. Of course your marketing will develop as you learn and mature in your niche, but it's essential you have a solid foundation on which to build.

Connecting It All Up

Here are some of the strategies and materials you'll need to establish yourself as an expert:

Client Attractive Website and Blog – By attractive I don't mean fancy graphics. I mean that it converts visitors into subscribers and clients.

Testimonials – Ask for testimonials from happy clients and buyers. Save all praise, positive reviews and testimonials to a file so that you can easily refer to them and sprinkle them throughout your marketing funnel and materials. Create a dedicated page on your website where you display all your testimonials. This is social proof at its finest.

Business Cards – Order just 250 and test out your USP and hook or angle. Asking relevant questions for your target market on the back of your business card draws people in. For example, a copywriter might ask 'Do you struggle to find the words to get your marketing message across?' Don't order thousands to get a good deal because the chances are you'll need to tweak your USP and 'hook' or 'angle' for connecting with prospects.

Coaching Service Webpage – You can offer one-to-one and/or group coaching programmes, depending on your experience and niche.

Special Reports – Publish online and/or in physical format. This is the fastest way of gaining credibility and publicity in your niche.

Ezine or Newsletter – This is my favourite way to stay in touch with my subscribers. If you're not already receiving my weekly ezine you can subscribe at www.RachelHenke.com and you'll experience exactly how a free ezine works and builds the relationship with your readers.

Your Own 'Signature System' – Once you've tested your market and are really clear on what you offer, I recommend you outline your own step-by-step system for your core service. From that you can create multiple information products such as e-books, home study programmes and/or an online membership site.

Coaching or Consulting Programmes – These can revolve around your system so that you have a clear coaching blueprint. A signature system will catapult you high above other coaches, consultants and entrepreneurs and establish you as an expert in your niche. It also clears away all confusion because you can focus on your system, and everything else becomes an avoidable distraction that will fade away. If it doesn't complement your system you can discard it.

Write Your Book or e-book – this may sound scary if you're not already an author, but it really doesn't need to be. Once you know your target market inside out and have created your own signature system, it's just a case of transferring your system into a book, guide or manual. This book stands alone or can serve as the companion to your coaching and product blueprint around which everything you offer for your niche revolves.

These days, the fastest and most efficient way to get your book into print is to publish it yourself. This is known as 'self publishing', not to be confused with 'vanity publishing', which is where you pay a company to publish a book for you. I'd steer clear of vanity publishers because they are more concerned with selling books to you than helping you to sell your books.

Self publishing is a brilliant option for experts to get their non-fiction book into print quickly. When you wait to be accepted by a publisher you can lose your flow and it might not be available on the market for months, if not years.

It all depends what kind of book you're writing, so consider your options carefully and make sure you have all the information.

You can sell your book online and off, keeping most of the profits. Whichever option you take, you'll need to do a lot of the marketing yourself anyway so why not keep more of the profits and have full control of your book?

The 'print on demand' business model is the most cost effective, low risk way to get your book into print and there are now many websites which provide this service. You can check out Amazon's service at: www.createspace.com or if you want to set yourself up as a publisher and assign an ISBN to your book, visit www.lightningsource.com or www.lightningsource.co.uk for more information.

If you prefer to just market your book online, you can package it as an e-book which is a fancy name for a pdf document and you can sell it through your marketing funnel and at your website.

Another option for you is to add your e-book to the Amazon Kindle store. You can find out more about how to do that here: http://kdp.amazon.com

Writing your first book as an expert may not bring you the big bucks in terms of royalties but it will establish you as an expert and is a wonderful tool for list building and relationship building with influential clients, organisations and other experts.

If you plan to offer workshops or seminars, having your own book and information products to sell at the back of the room is highly recommended.

As an author you become an author-ity and gain serious credibility and kudos.

People don't tend to throw books away, so you can use your book as a business card which will attract your best clients to you and give readers a low-cost sample of what it's like to work with you.

Selling your book online at your website is a great way to create a steady stream of income, gain the trust of your subscribers and offer a stepping stone into your higher-priced coaching programmes and information products.

Action Points

1. Create your Wordpress blog. Install it using the instructions from your hosting provider or tutorials from Optimise Press or other service. Alternatively outsource the installation to a web designer.

2. Connect free 'giveaway' or special report with your capture page, blog and email marketing system.

3. Review the marketing funnel plan and business model you mapped out in Chapter One and add in as much detail as you can for your website, signature system (optional) and attractive marketing materials.

SEVEN

ATTRACT HOT PROSPECTS INTO YOUR DATABASE

BUILDING YOUR LIST OR DATABASE is very exciting because, when done right, it represents an asset for you that will increase in value over time.

You may think your number one job is to be a coach, consultant or copywriter. Whilst delivering your product or service is important, marketing and building your list must be something you systemise and put on auto-pilot, if you ever want to escape the trap of trading time for money.

There are some mechanical and administrative things that you can outsource, but no one is going to know your target market like you.

This means that when you're positioning yourself as an expert using the internet, it's essential that you invest your time and energy into carving out your niche and connecting with your audience.

As a solo-entrepreneur or self-employed professional, you have a huge advantage over corporate companies because it's so easy for you to inject some personality and to really connect with your subscribers on a more personal level.

The rewards for doing this are that you'll be able to generate an endless stream of free or low paid subscribers signing up to hear from you on a regular basis.

You can do this by using a mix of social media and low cost advertising if you wish. The goal is to build a list of targeted subscribers who are in your niche market. It's not so much about large numbers as about quality, and attracting the right people into your database who will work with you or buy from you over and over again.

As an example, you might have a list of 10,000 subscribers who have signed up to your websites through a variety of unrelated offers. Or you could have a list of 1,000 who have signed up to receive something from you that directly relates to your niche and target market.

I know which list I'd prefer to be marketing to: definitely the smaller one. As a side note, your email marketing system will charge you for the service based on your total number of subscribers, so it really doesn't serve you to cobble together a list of people who are not actively seeking out what you have to offer.

You'll be crafting your marketing offers and they may be brilliant, but if they fall on deaf ears, your 'email open' and 'click through' rates will be very low. For example, you can't successfully sell information products for women to a list of baby boomer men. It seems obvious but take a close look at your marketing systems now and you may find you're not really targeting your niche as well as you could.

If you try to market highly specialised information to a generic group, the results will be poor. As a rule you'll find that people are willing to pay a lot more for specialised information, but of course it must be matched to a relevant list of responsive subscribers.

As we covered in earlier chapters, the best way to attract your ideal subscribers and buyers is to give away relevant information that answers their specific questions, in the form of a special report or free giveaway of some type.

By developing a strong 'hook' or angle for all your content at your website, the wrong people will automatically be sifted out before they even enter your marketing funnel. This is definitely great news because it means that all your focus and energy can go into marketing to, and working with, your ideal clients, partners or customers.

When you build a list of responsive subscribers and maintain it with care, you'll be paving the way to release yourself from marketing one-on-one, and moving into marketing to many with as little as one email per week.

Even if you love working with individual clients now, the day may come when you tire and crave more time freedom to pursue other projects. Working one-on-one with clients, although the only thing most coaches have ever known, can be very time consuming and restrictive.

Building your list gives you an asset for the future that will become your safety net. If you focus and consistently grow a targeted list, it won't be long before you can send out one email and make hundreds, if not thousands of dollars, depending on the price and quality of the products you market.

The amazing thing about having your own targeted list is that by opting into receive your email tips or ezine (newsletter), your subscribers are giving you permission to market to them over and over again. This is known as 'permission marketing' and is a phrase coined by the innovative and prolific marketing expert, Seth Godin.

Based on the proven advertising research that most people need to see a marketing message seven or more times before buying, it makes sense that most of your readers will not be ready to buy from you immediately. For that reason you want to entice them onto your mailing list so that when they are ready to use a product or service for your niche, they come to you as the go-to-expert.

It really is quite simple. It's not rocket science, but there are so many options and things being hurled at us online that you might think it more complicated than it actually is.

Your Marketing Gameplan

The key is to create your own marketing game plan which you stick to and focus on each day, week, month and quarter. Building your list is about putting some simple little systems in place that will work for you over and over. As the great Jim Rohn, used to say, 'it's easy to do and easy not to do'. You'll look back in a few years and be so grateful that you built your list, so let's get going shall we?

There are many ways to build your list or database but here I'll cover the most effective methods that you can choose from:

Warm Letter

When you launch your new business or programmes you can make a very fast start by contacting the people who already know, like and trust you, and ask for their help.

Send a letter of introduction, explaining what you're up to with details of your programmes or services and asking for your contacts to pass it on to anyone they know who might be looking for this kind of service. Personalise the letters and send them by snail mail rather than email wherever possible.

This is a very low pressure and professional way of explaining to your friends, family and contacts what you have to offer without 'selling them'. Make sure you include your USP here so your expert status is obvious at a glance, and you become the go-to-expert in their mind for this service.

This works particularly well for service businesses so be sure to also make a list of all the people who have expressed interest in working with you in the past but have never gotten started with you. Touch base with them and send them some information about your latest programmes or services. This can lead to highly converting referrals where people come to you ready to buy or work with you.

Memory Joggers for your warm letter:

- Check your email address book and outlook
- Go through your mobile phone contacts
- Remember your online and offline address and phone books
- Old diaries
- Business cards you've collected
- Skype contacts
- Old work colleagues – LinkedIn and professional groups
- Other social network friends

Groups and Forums

Let's say you are looking to attract working mums who would like to work from home and be around for their kids more. You can easily find many online groups for mums: search on Google for forums and groups using your keywords; identify two to three groups and begin commenting and interacting with the forum or group members. You'll also be able to find the best groups for you to join on Facebook or LinkedIn.

Specific forums are very effective. Let's say you are a weight loss coach and you identify several active forums -- you can check this by seeing that there are a significant number of members and recent comments in the forum – all you need to do is read the guidelines so you know how the forum operates, introduce yourself and comment on any threads or conversations that grab your attention. A great way of generating interest is by asking or answering questions on your expert topic.

You can ask people what they'd like to know, thus positioning yourself as an expert without being salesy or pushy. Or you can volunteer answers on existing threads.

The trick is to always come from a place of giving value (I keep repeating this as it's so important) and don't push your products or services. People will click on your profile to find out more about you because they will be compelled to when you interact this way.

Always include a direct link to your webpage where they can sign up for your special report or giveaway at the bottom of your forum or group posts, wherever permitted. Remember the social media sins and don't be tempted to post your link all over the place because it will work against you.

The key to succeeding in forums and groups is to revisit often so that people in your target market get to know you. If you choose this as a method, it is free and works well, but you do need to be disciplined with it and check in each day or every couple of days for best results.

On the bright side it is a residual method, meaning that your posts and links will remain there for as long as the forum exists. Most forums and groups are picked up by search engines, unless they are private, so you will be leaving a sticky trail of expert posts on your keywords.

On your Google account set up a 'Google alert' for your keyword and niche search terms. You'll be notified each time someone posts about your expert topic.

Facebook – start a Group and/or Business Page

Facebook pages and groups are often picked up on by search engines and it's relatively easy to appear on the first page of Google with an active group or page. Creating a group around your expert topic is therefore an effective method for generating leads both from within the social network and via keywords on the search engines.

I consider having a Facebook Page a must for positioning yourself as an expert – we covered that in Chapter Four.

Twitter

Twitter is the micro-blogging site that allows you to ping your words of wisdom and links to your new content all over your universe. Twitter is an amazing way to pick up new subscribers and build relationships with your target market. Make sure your niche keywords are in your bio and you tweet several times per day. Using the tips in Chapters Four and Five will keep this quick and simple for you.

LinkedIn

LinkedIn is a wonderful place to network and answer questions on your expert topic. As with all networking on forums and groups, first create a rich and detailed profile so that when people come back to check you out they are not disappointed. Scatter your niche keywords throughout your profile where relevant so that you will have more chance of appearing in searches.

Search for groups on LinkedIn and start to network and make friends with people in your target market. Always have your landing page and free giveaway link prominent on your profile and if you consistently interact you'll be generating high quality prospects into your targeted list.

Always focus on benefits, not features. For instance, your visitors will be much more interested in what you can do for them as opposed to how many certificates you have, so be specific when creating your profile.

LinkedIn Answers

If LinkedIn serves your target market, this is a section you will want to take advantage of. The social media sites change their layout so often that I won't attempt to explain where it is, but if you search in the different tabs in your profile, you'll find the Answers section.

Here you can ask and answer questions. Choose your subject and start answering questions. LinkedIn, showcase the best answers as 'Top Experts'. Need I say more?

If you visit often you'll be in an excellent position to be approached with invitations to be featured as an expert in articles, books and teleseminars and webinars (online seminars).

These methods take time but are free so represent a great choice for getting started and you can do just a little bit each day and build on that.

A Word of Warning

There are many forums, groups and online networks, so keep an eye out for the ones that specifically match your target market and needs. Don't overdo it or you'll burn out. It's better to pick two or three forums or groups where you regularly participate than to spread yourself too thin trying to be an expert in them all.

More Ways To Build Your Expert Status

Once you've established your presence and mastered two or three groups or forums, you can add in others to the mix. Wherever you can create a content rich profile and link up your Twitter feeds so that you can reach more places without physically being there, this is a bonus. Based on results and feedback you can decide where your time will be best invested for manual commenting and networking.

Articles

This is one of the tried and true list-building methods and, although some people may think it's had its day, the truth is this works just as well as it ever did. Posting articles to popular article directories such as ezinearticles.com, articlesbase.com and ehow.com is one of the foundation methods I use for driving high quality traffic to my websites.

You can also approach relevant physical magazines to publish your articles, which can drive targeted traffic from offline to online at no cost.

This method is easy and free to do. As we covered in the last chapter, you create one article and post it to many places to increase your exposure, and to leverage that piece of content.

This also creates what's known as a 'back link' to your website which in turn boosts its rankings in the search engines. Having many articles on article directories positions you as an expert and has an accumulative and residual effect. Paid advertising is instant, but when it's over, it's over. These free methods I'm sharing with you will continue working for you forever and will not disappear overnight like most of the latest gimmicky marketing tricks.

Tele-seminars

Turn one of your articles, talks or special reports into a free tele-seminar. This just means people will be able to dial in to listen to you covering some of your expert content. Here you'll want to cover the 'why and the what' but not go into full detail on the how. The how will be what you cover in your paid products and services. Of course you won't be able to cover all the details in a short tele-seminar anyway.

You'll need what's known as a 'bridge line' so that people can call into a specified number to hear your call. Alternatively you can just record yourself covering the content and post it at your website.

This is a great way to generate hot leads because you set it up so that new visitors and listeners must opt-in to your list to receive access to the live tele-seminar or audio. You can create a lot of buzz around this with your blog and social sites, and also ask your subscribers to pass on the invitation to their friends.

Webinars

These are similar to tele-seminars, but you provide

slides as a visual presentation. The benefit of a webinar is that people can log in at no charge and from anywhere with just an internet connection. There are many services that offer the facility to host webinars and some of them can be quite costly, so compare services and find the one that suits you best. As with tele-seminars, set it up so that your listeners must opt-in to your list to receive details.

Ezine or Newsletter

Ezines can also be great list-builders. When you publish your ezine or newsletter, most email providers automatically generate an RSS feed which posts your content to an online archive. You can add the RSS feed to your Wordpress website in a widget so that visitors can click and have a sample of your ezine before they sign up. Ask your technical helper or web designer to do it for you if you're not familiar with it.

You can also ping out the ezine archive link to your social networks to encourage new subscribers to join your list to receive your weekly ezine to their inbox.

Submit your ezine to ezine directories. Do a search for ezine directories and follow the submission instructions.

Ezines are the best way to keep your subscribers and when a visitor downloads your special report, let them know they will also receive a complimentary subscription to your ezine.

Blog Posts

This is my favourite way of gaining new subscribers to my list and in my experience, the absolutely most time-efficient and easiest to do.

Post your article or blog post between one and three times per week and link up your blog with all your social media sites. You can usually do this by adding your Blog RSS feed to the social networks so it automatically announces your new blog posts.

When you publish a new blog post or other piece of content, it's time to let the world know. It's similar to owning a newspaper and announcing it to the world, so whip out your virtual loudspeaker to send your content whizzing on its way. Always notify your followers on your social networks. Social media is changing so fast you'll need to adapt as you go, but the trick is to link them up wherever you can to save time and automate the process.

Blog Comments

Search for authority blogs at Blogsearch.google.com in your niche and comment on them. Much like in the forums or groups, give value by offering your unique viewpoint on the blog post. Include your website domain so that people reading the blog who find your comment valuable can click through to your website. This is also a great way of gaining the attention of the blog publisher, and the gateway to becoming a guest blogger.

Be a Guest Blogger

Search for authority blogs in your niche and begin to follow the blog and submit valuable comments to build a relationship with the blog publisher. Contact them to ask whether they accept guest blog posts. This is a great way of getting your article in front of thousands of people in your target market, and also creates a powerful back link to your website.

You never know who it will attract into your world so don't underestimate the power of great content on your expert topic. This is a proven strategy for bringing your work to the attention of key influencers in your field of expertise. You position yourself for joint ventures and strategic alliances with people who would otherwise never have heard of you.

Organic Search Listings

Your website appearing on the first page of Google and other search listings is a natural result of creating lots of relevant content containing the niche keywords you identified in Chapter Two. Over time you'll find your articles, blogs and videos appearing in search listings which will generate targeted traffic and hot prospects to your website. When you plan your content bear in mind to keep it tightly focussed around your profitable keywords so that each time you post a new article or video you are one step closer to dominating your niche.

SEO or Search Engine Optimisation

SEO is what you need to do to your website to help it list high in the search listings. Your keywords need to be added into your website and you can do it yourself or have a web designer do it for you.

This is very easy to do on Wordpress and there are specific plugins that you upload to your site which add some keyword juice to your site and help it appear in the listings.

For each individual blog post and other piece of content you publish, always submit it with the relevant keywords and this will help it to appear in the top listings for those keywords. It takes a few extra minutes but will be the difference between your post being found, and it just being another piece of neglected content clogging up the web.

Video Marketing

It's very easy these days to create short videos and you can be as creative as your imagination allows. To attract hot prospects into your list you can create a series of 'how to' videos for your expert topic. You can use a FLIP video camera that allows you to upload your videos straight to your computer. If you're not comfortable getting in front of the camera you can create a PowerPoint presentation and have your web designer show you how to turn it into a video.

Set it up as a free giveaway so your visitors need to opt in on the capture page or blog to access your free videos.

To attract new visitors to your website, submit your videos to popular video-sharing sites such as YouTube and Viddler. Always include your URL for the exact page you want them to go to after watching the video. Put it at the top in the description section and include a keyword rich description that matches the video.

This is very powerful but time intensive so you can outsource it to an assistant or teenage helper if you have one.

Use Tubemogul.com to upload your video to multiple sites with one click.

Podcasts

Podcasts are like having your own radio show. Audio is hot and draws people to you in the same way as video. You can create your own short podcasts and submit the link to iTunes.

Select your category carefully and include a keyword rich description. When someone subscribes to your podcast feed, all of your future podcasts will be downloaded automatically to their computer and they can listen to them online or with an MP3 player. Make sure to include a call to action explaining how to claim your special report or free giveaway at the end of the podcast. This is how you attract them into your list or database.

Networking

We're focused on online strategies here, but nonetheless, as already mentioned, I urge you not to overlook offline marketing. When you're out and about or attending networking events you can ask people who are a match for what you have to offer if it's ok for you to add them to your ezine list to receive weekly tips on your expert topic. This is a great, no pressure way to introduce them to what you offer.

Always ask permission; never just add them, because that is considered spamming. Keep the concept of 'permission marketing' in mind and you'll be fine.

Depending on what type of business you have there are probably many different networking associations you can join in your local area. A couple of the big global organisation meetings are BNI and Chamber of Commerce.

These offer an effective strategy for gaining referral business as you meet regularly with other business people and focus on exchanging referrals. They are membership based and require a long term commitment to be of value to you as the relationships your build with local business owners will take some time to mature.

This is a perfect example of a method to include on your marketing game plan because you'll know in advance that you have an effective strategy in place for one morning per week or whatever the schedule is for the networking group.

Do a Google search for other networking groups, seminars, workshops and events in your area. Even if you focus primarily on the internet methods it can still be refreshing to get out and meet other business owners.

By attending local, national or even overseas conferences related to your field of expertise you can get to know some of the top influencers so that you can form possible joint ventures and even request testimonials for your products and books. The coffee break conversations in hallways at big events are often the inspiration for many lucrative partnerships and Aha! moments so don't hide behind your computer 24/7.

Press Releases

If you're working with a publicist or media expert they will handle this for you, but if you're doing it all yourself this is a great way to get the word out about your new book, company, method or system. Google the press release submission sites and follow the guidelines for creating and submitting your press release. You can submit them free, or pay for extra exposure. The idea is that you're announcing something new and exciting. Include your keywords so that your press releases are picked up in organic searches for your niche.

Speaking and Events

The finer details of this are beyond the scope of this book, but as an overview this is a great way to quickly establish yourself as an expert in your local or national market.

The easiest way to do this is to turn your special report or tele-seminar into a signature talk. This could correspond with the outline of your book or signature system which we covered earlier. By taking the key points of your expertise you save yourself hundreds of hours trying to constantly recreate ways to present your information to your target market.

As an expert you need to *specialise* and become known for the main benefit that your target market receives as a result of working with you or buying your products. Repetition is the fast track to mastering anything quickly, so your job is to teach the fundamentals by packaging them in attractive multiple formats. The most efficient way to do this is to use your signature talk, tele-seminar, online content and book as the centrepiece around which revolve all your related services and products.

Sweet. Do you see how it takes all the confusion out of the equation? Yes, there is a lot of work to do to set all this up but once you have the foundation in place you can build on it and everything you do from then on is focused and productive to establish you as an expert.

Timothy Ferriss is a great example of how to become an expert and generate huge online buzz for your brand. In his bestselling book *The 4 Hour Work Week,* he gives some tips on how to be perceived as a top expert in four weeks.

Here's a summary of some of the tips that I found most relevant for self-employed professionals and solo-entrepreneurs:

1. Join two or three related trade organisations with official sounding names.

2. Read the three top-selling books on your topic

3. Give a free one to three hour seminar at the closest well- known university, using posters to advertise.

4. Offer to write an article for trade magazines and mention what you did in tips 1 to 3 so that you establish credibility.

5. Interview an expert, write it up in an article and offer it to the trade magazines

On the subject of interviewing experts, this is a fast and easy way to create high value content for your website by recording the interview and producing what's known as an audio MP3 file which you can copy to a CD and/or post on your website. There are many services that provide a way to do this and it's one of the easiest ways to create your own free or paid-for information product or series of interviews.

Strategic Alliances

This is where you identify people who serve a similar target market as you, and you develop ways to help each other out. As you gain confidence and create more products and services you'll want to always be looking for ways to add in more streams of income. You can do what's known as a 'joint venture', a partnership with these key people to create products and services together and split the profits. For list-building you can cross-promote each other's tele-seminars or write for each other's blogs. There are endless ways of partnering to help each other grow your lists and reach people you just wouldn't be able to reach otherwise.

Paid Advertising

With so many no cost ways available to build your list, paid advertising can be overlooked. However it offers an instant method of generating traffic and targeted prospects into your list which organic search engine listings just can't do.

Here are some of the methods you might want to consider and test:

- **Google Pay Per Click** – get some specific training on how to set up campaigns using your profitable keywords. You already laid the groundwork for your campaigns in Chapter Two.

- **Facebook Advertising** – similar to pay per click but exclusively on Facebook. These adverts work particularly well to attract publicity for your online and offline events.

- **Banner Adverts** – banners in the form of html messages which you pay to have shown on high traffic websites in your niche.

- **Online/Offline Classified Adverts** – lineage adverts in online and physical publications.

- **Solo Adverts** – you pay to have adverts shown in other people's ezines/newsletters for your target market.

For paid advertising it is even more essential that you have a highly converting marketing funnel with a compelling marketing message and free giveaway in place *first*. You can get some great results but you need to study these methods individually and I recommend you add them in one at a time to your marketing mix, to avoid overwhelm.

Always set your marketing budget before you start and make sure you understand how to limit the amount you spend per day or per advert. Test each method carefully and use Google Analytics on your web pages so you can track all of your traffic and conversions.

Use a link tracking programme in any adverts that you place, so that you know which adverts are working for you and which are a waste of money. This can be quite complicated so get some specialised help rather than guessing, because it will cost you more if you don't know what you're doing. Ignorance is not bliss.

Affiliate Programme

By offering a good affiliate programme, you can have a free army of entrepreneurs out promoting your products for you. An affiliate programme means that you allow your affiliates to promote your products and you split the commission with them when someone buys through their affiliate link. This means you only pay them when a sale is generated. It's a great way to speed up sales but it's also a fabulous method for attracting hot prospects into your list. You'll need an affiliate marketing service for this so that it is all automated and tracked for you on auto-pilot.

Action Points

1. Research the different methods here and add the ones that appeal to you most into your marketing game plan. Choosing a mix of *steady* and *instant* methods works best so, for instance, social networking is a steady list-builder but hosting a tele-seminar can be an instant list-builder.

2. Consider implementing some of Tim Ferriss' tips on positioning yourself as an expert.

EIGHT

CONVERT PROSPECTS INTO CLIENTS, BUYERS AND OPPORTUNITIES

THE INTERNET BRINGS SO MUCH opportunity to us at the click of a mouse. For that reason it's critical that you understand that for the majority of businesses there is a need to integrate 'high tech' with 'high touch'.

What I mean by this is that you use the internet tools to sort your potential clients, customers or prospects for you. This is the high tech element, but to be successful you *must* also sprinkle the high touch element into the mix.

Whether you're a coach, consultant, speaker, network marketer, artist, or other business owner you're going to have to connect with your potential clients or customers.

Technology has brought with it so many wonderful benefits but it can never replace the heart that you bring to your relationships.

So it's all about giving value and building trust with individuals in your target market or niche. People buy from, and do business with, those whom they like and trust. I'm missing out the usual 'know' bit because when you position yourself with the steps

I've given you here, people don't really need to 'know' you to buy from you but they do need to trust you.

If you take the steps outlined in the chapters in this book, it won't be long before it seems as though you are everywhere at once. You'll be reaching out to your potential clients with your compelling message and attracting a lot of people into your marketing funnel on auto-pilot.

Plan Your Conversion Process

How you convert your prospects into paying customers or clients will depend very much on exactly which type of business model you have. For many, you will need to pick up the phone and follow up with the people who opted into your marketing funnel and requested more information about a specific programme or service.

Set up everything so your prospects call you where possible, but until you've got more business than you can handle don't wait around just thinking people are going to be chasing after you. If they include their phone number on a form at your website, they are giving you, or someone on your team, permission to call them, so don't disappoint.

If you're building an online information business with no coaching or consulting practice, then you won't need to call them. When you're getting started online, or are transitioning from traditional methods to an internet based business, I recommend you keep the things in place that are working for you now, and do a gradual switch to your new business model.

It's a happy day when you start to receive lots of lead notifications in your inbox. A lead notification is an email message that your email provider will send you each time you have a new subscriber to your database or list.

It's up to you whether you want to include a telephone number field for all of your subscribers to complete, or whether you'll just collect their name and email. It really depends on what you offer and how much time you have for calling people.

The difference between success and failure is determined by what you do with your leads. We'll look at this from the client attraction point of view because that's the most proactive approach. What you do with your lead will depend on how it came to you and what process you put your prospect through before they requested information from you.

If you follow the process I outline for you here, and your prospect has come through your 'client attractive' marketing funnel, they will be a red hot lead for you. If your marketing funnel and website are set up right, some of the following credibility factors will already have worked in your favour before you even speak to them:

- They may feel like they already know you a little – how well depends on the quality of information they've received from you so far

- They already trust you as an expert in your niche – to what degree depends on what they have seen at your website

- They are definitely seeing you as a solution provider because they've requested a call with you, or are calling you directly

- They have clicked around your blog and been motivated to take the next step with you

- They may have had all their questions answered in the materials at your website

- They may already have identified a specific programme or product that they want to go forward with and be ready to buy

Do you see why this is a red hot prospect for you? Compare this to the old style of doing business where you speak to potential clients who just got your listing out of the newspaper or phone book.

You don't need to spend a lot of time building credibility with them and selling yourself because the prospect has sold themselves before calling you.

Outline your programmes on your website and point the readers of your special report there as a next step. On that page you can have a sign up form where they qualify themselves still further and request a call with you.

I recommend that you resist launching into answering questions and explaining your programmes straight away. Instead, schedule an appointment with them and send them an email or give them your programme web page to visit and review before your call. This will ensure they have reviewed your programmes properly before your call and will allow you to protect your time by scheduling calls only with the serious candidates who are a good match for your programmes.

All you need to do is find out about their situation and what challenges they have. Listen to them and take detailed notes. It's good to have specific questions to use here so you are always prepared before your call. After you've listened and understood the caller's challenges, answer any questions about working with you, and walk them through your programmes.

Warning: Do not coach them for free at this point because you'll lose them. Why should they pay to work with you if you do it at no charge?

The Consultative Approach

The 'consultative approach' is the whole process of them coming to you and you listening and advising them, as a consultant does.

The 'gentle close' comes into play at the end where they are considering your programmes. Rather than selling them hard, which is what most people expect, you surprise them and give them further confidence by asking them casually, which programme they can see themselves going for if they do decide to get started with you.

Listen and affirm their choice as a good one. Ask them when they see themselves getting started and, if they are ready, wrap it up by congratulating them on their decision and taking payment.

Voila. You have yourself a new Ideal Client.

This way of connecting with your potential clients is lovely because it's something that we can all do. If you hate being salesy, and convincing people to do business with you makes you squirm, this is for you.

The 'consultative approach' empowers you to help people make the right decision for them by setting everything up for them to come to you, ready to buy or sign up with you.

For an internet based model where you provide services or products that can be marketed and purchased solely through email and an online shopping cart, use the above 'client process' as a guide but customise it for your online steps.

Draw out your process and implement the online steps for your prospects and customers to follow.

Whichever specific business model you operate, you are building your email list and gathering leads on auto-pilot every day so that people have an opportunity to experience your free report and ezine, as well as to purchase lower cost products from you.

Not everyone is going to be a match for your high end products or coaching and consulting programmes but many will still want to buy from you if you offer your information in different formats and at various price points.

In the short term you'll be able to easily convert your hot leads into clients by speaking or connecting with only those best suited to your programmes. In the long term you'll be staying in touch with potentially thousands of quality prospects for your target market, many of whom over time will buy from you or join your programmes when the time is right for them.

There is no more of that awful 'buy or die', attitude once you set up your website and marketing funnel to focus on giving value, without pressuring people to work with you or buy from you on the spot.

Building Credibility Trust

Your weekly ezine will also help you to achieve high client or customer conversion as it will continue to build the relationship, credibility and trust between you over the long term.

Your ezine (newsletter) or email marketing is an essential component of client conversion because it will enable you to keep your subscribers for many years so that they receive multiple opportunities to do business with you.

It's very easy to maintain once you've sorted out the first one and have your template. As covered in Chapter Four, I favour Aweber and use a template that I've customised for my own use. There are hundreds of templates to choose from but if none suit your requirements you can outsource it to a web designer who will customise it for you in a few clicks.

A plain email newsletter works too but is quite old fashioned and not very eye catching. An html email gets better click-throughs than a plain text email. By adding in your website graphic (with your photo on) you'll be branding yourself as an expert while staying in touch with your readers.

A template also allows you to highlight certain products and services without having to have very long emails, which don't work so well considering most of us are overwhelmed with all the information coming at us online.

Whatever template you choose, it's critical for success that you set a publishing schedule for your ezine. Once per week is best and is the minimum for successful prospect to client or customer conversion. You can email more but it will be a fine line between too much of a good thing and not enough for your subscribers to really connect with you.

I tend to email once or twice a week depending what's going on. Your ezine is easy to create because you'll probably be creating a blog post or article at least once a week as a marketing method anyway.

You post that in your ezine, or link your article section to your blog post. Both work well so it's an individual preference. I alternate between the two, but either way you'll want to give your ezine readers a good reason to click on links to revisit your website or blog regularly. While they are there they'll be able to check out your programmes and products.

My best tip for you on this is to remember to always be honest and authentic because your readers will pick up inconsistencies and if they don't trust you they will not work with you or buy from you: end of story.

My ezine goes out each week come thunder or plague. Your readers will trust you more when they see you deliver consistently. What starts as a subscriber for your free information may turn into a paying client or customer when you stay in touch.

Highlight your main programmes and products in a section of your ezine, and you can also include reviews for affiliate products that compliment your expert niche and will allow you to generate more streams of automated income.

The ezine is a drip-feeding strategy which builds tremendous credibility because you become the trusted advisor and expert in your niche. Many ezines get between 20% to 50% open rates so it's an amazing way to keep your subscribers with you for years to come. This is the magic formula for engaging a loyal 'tribe'.

Action Points

1. Outline your client conversion or online buying process on paper. Decide on the specific steps you want your prospects to take so that you can qualify them and 'cherry pick' your clients or projects.

2. Think about how you can package your products and services into programmes that create recurring income and exciting new passive income streams.

3. Begin or optimise your ezine. Weekly is best but fortnightly can work too if you're worried about finding the time. The most important thing is to be seen to deliver on your promises so decide on an ezine schedule and stick to it.

NINE

SYSTEMISE YOUR MARKETING SO IT WORKS ON AUTO-PILOT

YOUR HEAD IS PROBABLY SPINNING by now with all the amazing possibilities and ways to grow your business using the internet. We're on the last chapter and here I'm going to give you the exact formula to create your personalised plan and put your marketing on auto-pilot.

Is that a sigh of relief I hear? Yes I know how overwhelming all of this can be, which is the reason I created my own system and marketing game plan. I was tired of trying to reinvent the wheel and having to put so much effort and thought into my marketing each week.

I was burned out with networking and one-to-one marketing. I had a great message but it wasn't reaching enough people. Perhaps you can relate to that.

My goal with my business is to give value to my target market but also to create true freedom for myself and to show my clients and customers how to do the same. True freedom, in my view, consists of both time and financial freedom.

I wanted enough time to do all the things I love to do with my life and enough money so that I don't have to think about it very often. I see money as just a tool for us to live the best life we are destined to live, and the fastest way to automate your income is to automate your marketing.

Let's wrap up here by getting into the nitty-gritty of how to create your personalised marketing game plan.

If you haven't yet downloaded your *'Marketing Game Plan and Social Media Toolkit'* special bonus, please do so now as this will provide you with a template for your marketing game plan and social media strategy: www.RachelHenke.com/the-niche-expert-book-gift

To design your own marketing game plan flick back to Chapter Seven and select up to ten methods for attracting hot prospects into your database.

Choose at least seven that you feel most aligned with. It's quite normal if you have some nervous butterflies in your tummy about hosting your own tele-seminar or speaking to a group. If the thought of it terrifies you and doesn't excite you then choose seven from the other methods first.

You can grow into doing some of the other things as your confidence and expertise in your niche grow. Choose some things that seem fairly easy to you, because we're all different. One person might find it exciting to create a short video whereas another might find writing an article much easier.

I recommend you select at least seven methods to add into your marketing game plan over the next six to 12 months, because if you only focus on one or two methods you're leaving your success too much to chance.

If you only market on Facebook and Twitter and your Facebook account gets deleted in error or closed down, you'll be stuck without a flow of leads for your business. It's too risky to only focus on a few methods.

Some of the methods build your list at a steady pace and others provide instant subscribers such as tele-seminars, webinars and other events.

A combination of both types works the best and you can mix it up as you gain confidence with the different methods.

Nevertheless, I suggest you begin with just two or three methods and master them first before you go on to implement all seven. How fast you go depends on how much time you allocate in your marketing schedule. This is how you create an actionable game plan that will become your marketing system on auto-pilot.

Let's say you have no ezine or email marketing system in place so you pick that as your first method to implement. Set it up and schedule it for a specific day of the week. It will take you a while to get familiar with how to create your weekly ezine, and what flows best for you, so focus on that first before moving on to other methods. Getting one thing at a time working well is better than floundering with seven all at once.

Do you recall in the first chapter we talked about the success mindset for becoming an expert? An action point was to create your marketing schedule and allocate specific chunks of time for your marketing activities. This is where you'll need that information because you'll be adding in specific daily, weekly, monthly and quarterly activities to your schedule.

Let's say you send your ezine out each Wednesday. If you're anything like other entrepreneurs, sometimes you can get sidetracked by the flow of ideas and projects coming at you.

By scheduling your marketing activities you create systems to support you and to keep you accountable. Rather than waking up on Wednesday thinking, 'grrrr what can I do this week to attract more clients or customers?' you'll be able to simply refer to your game plan for Wednesdays, and publish your ezine in the chunk of time already allocated.

If you've been implementing all of the action points, you will have leads starting to flow in consistently already. Now is the time to systemise your efforts so you can work less and cherry pick the clients and projects you love.

Begin creating your game plan and scheduling each activity. As an example, if you want to do some offline networking, schedule in your weekly or monthly networking events.

For your blogging and articles, schedule in a time to write at least one each week and submit them to multiple article sites and/or publications. You can outsource the submission easily to save time. If you prefer you can create videos and submit those instead.

If you want to contribute your articles to other blogs or publications that your target market reads, then allocate a weekly session where you contact the relevant website owners, publications or associations.

If you have a client-focused business you'll also need to block out the client time you need.

Once you have created your game plan, transfer your daily, weekly, monthly and quarterly marketing activities to a one-year wall planner and/or diary. This is a visual reminder for you to commit to these activities and also helps you to think in a big way.

It's so much more exciting and effective to have a big, organised marketing plan and simple strategy for the year than just taking it day by day.

These systems run by themselves and you can outsource as much as you like once you are generating more income, as a result of growing your business with your marketing game plan.

I recommend you keep doing the things that have

been working for you until now, but weed out the things that haven't and replace them with the new methods.

Track and test everything you can. Use Google Analytics on your website to monitor traffic sources and visitors. Keep a track of where your best clients or leads come from; always ask people where and how they found you. Once you know which methods work best for you, you can put more energy into those and discard methods that are less effective.

If you've started with an online business you may want to develop your own coaching programmes, signature system, workshops and/or information home study courses around your expert topic. The sky is the limit when you become an expert in your niche and you can design your business to suit your perfect lifestyle. Have fun.

Action Points

1. Complete your marketing game plan.

2. Create your social media strategy.

3. Check back and implement any exercises you missed.

Congratulations on completing *The Niche Expert*. I've enjoyed showing you how to become the 'go to' expert in your niche and look forward to hearing how you get on.

I'll leave you with the perfect quote for *The Niche Expert*, from Martha Stewart:

> *'Build your business success around something that you love – something that is inherently and endlessly interesting to you'.*

Yours in success!
Rachel Henke
***The Niche Expert* Coach**

www.rachelhenke.com
www.facebook.com/rachelhenkefan
www.twitter.com/rachelhenke

P.S. All the important resources from this book are listed for your convenience on the next page.

RESOURCES AND LINKS

What's Next?

***The Niche Expert* Coaching and Mentoring Programmes**

www.RachelHenke.com/coaching

Your Free Gift 'Marketing Game Plan and Social Media Toolkit'

www.RachelHenke.com/the-niche-expert-book-gift

Ask *The Niche Expert* Coach a question by email

Rachel@Rachelhenke.com

Home Study *Niche Expert* Modules:

www.Rachelhenke.com/internet-bootcamp

Latest Resources:

www.RachelHenke.com/recommends

Useful Links

Wordpress Optimise Press Theme

Easy, low cost and quick set up of capture pages, sales pages, blog and marketing funnels
www.nanacast.com/vp/97647/126367

Wordpress Self Hosted Blog

www.wordpress.org

Email and e-zine Marketing Solution

www.aweber.com/?367818

Domain Provider

www.GoDaddy.com

Website Hosting

www.Hostgator.com

Internet Copywriting Service

www.RachelHenke.com/Copywriting

Twitter Applications

www.Twitter.com
www.Hootsuite.com
www.Tweetdeck.com
Update Social Networks – www.Ping.fm
Share videos with one submission –
www.Tubemogul.com

Social Networks and Video Sites

www.LinkedIn.com
www.YouTube.com
www.Viddler .com
www.Ecademy.com
www.Facebook.com
www.Twitter.com
www.Plaxo.com

Article Submission Sites

www.ezinearticles.com

www.articlesbase.com

www.amazines.com

Book Publishing Sites

www.lightningsource.com or

www.lightningsource.co.uk

www.createspace.com

kdp.amazon.com

Find authority blogs

www.blogsearch.google.com

Find the right people to follow

www.search.twitter.com

Check out your online brand

www.123people.com or www.123people.co.uk

Set up your account here for multiple online services
referred to throughout the book – www.google.com

Books

Outliers, Malcolm Gladwell. Little, Brown and
Company, 2008

Tribes, Seth Godin. Piatkus, 2008

Confidence in High Heels, Rachel Henke.
www.confidenceinhighheels.com, 2010

Crush It, Gary Vaynerchuk. Harperstudio, 2009

The Four Hour Work Week, Tim Ferriss. Vermilion, 2007

The Wealthy Author, Joe Gregory. Bookshaker, 2009

RACHEL HENKE

 Rachel Henke is an author, coach and founder of *The Niche Expert System*, teaching solo and home based entrepreneurs how to become the go-to expert in their niche to attract their perfect clients, publicity and big opportunities online whilst working less, charging more, making a difference doing what they love!

Rachel's marketing journey began in 2003 when she discovered the home business arena but it was in 2007 that her love affair with the internet began and she says, 'I experienced one of those electrifying aha moments when I realised that even with cows for neighbours in this tiny rural village I could build a global business with the internet.'

As a result of switching her niche and experiencing all of the confusion that goes with it, she wrote *The Niche Expert*, especially for entrepreneurs who want to stand out from the internet crowd and not get trampled under the 'cyber' foot.

Learn more at www.RachelHenke.com

4019814R00103

Printed in Germany
by Amazon Distribution
GmbH, Leipzig